NORWICH
IN THE
GILDED
AGE

THE ROSE CITY'S MILLIONAIRES' TRIANGLE

Black Stone on Caset now, called BS apartments

PATRICIA F. STALEY

Charleston | London

THE
History
PRESS

Published by The History Press
Charleston, SC 29403
www.historypress.net

First published 2014

Manufactured in the United States

ISBN 978.1.62619.247.8

Library of Congress CIP data applied for.

CONTENTS

Contents

PREFACE

During the nineteenth century, Norwich, Connecticut, was an extraordinary place for not only its wealth but also the confluence of extraordinary people who lived in the city. For their homes, they gravitated toward a triangle-shaped mile that became the city's most fashionable neighborhood in the last half of the century. Norwich boasted a competitive advantage economically because of its location between New York and Boston and the combination of a short, navigable river with a sheltered harbor and smaller rivers to power factories; a beautiful setting where people wanted to live; an entrepreneurial culture that fostered the creation of local businesses; and a civic culture that prompted local residents to benefit the community by developing infrastructure (steamboat, railroad, etc.) and educational, religious and cultural facilities.

Most of the wealthy families of Norwich were manufacturers, but merchants, bankers, railroad executives and lawyers were also among their number. They had great wealth and used it to benefit the city, building a library, a social service agency, a hospital and a private secondary school that rivaled colleges for the education provided, all of which still serve the city today. They used their own money to establish steamboat lines and railroads (one to New London, one to Worcester) that profited their businesses but also made Norwich a crossroads for travelers and goods moving between New York and Boston.

They were both generous and prompt in financial support as the Civil War began. Connecticut's Governor William A. Buckingham was their

Norwich neighbor and friend. When he called for troops, they offered financial support for the soldiers' families, many of whom would be losing a breadwinner. The governor himself used his personal credit to ensure that Connecticut's volunteer militia would be well and properly equipped.

It's difficult to think of historical figures as people who had families and lives outside their businesses. Perhaps it is because the history books tend to focus on their achievements and generally don't mention the obstacles they had to overcome and the difficulties they faced in their personal lives.

In Norwich, many of the millionaires' residences are still standing, and this project began as a personal mission to match houses with owners and their businesses. My interest was further piqued when I learned that William Slater's wife had lived in the house my family occupied for some years, which wasn't far from the Millionaires' Triangle. Ultimately, the mission became to tell and preserve the millionaires' stories.

Information for this volume was compiled from a large number of resources, including nineteenth-century maps of Norwich and city directories. Addresses given in the book have two numbers because Washington Street and Broadway were renumbered in 1885–86. The higher numbers remain valid in the twenty-first century.

Researching the millionaire families required careful checking of birth and death dates for each name. Children were commonly given the name of a parent or close relative. For example, there are three William A. Buckinghams (the governor, his nephew and a grandnephew) and at least four Augusta Greenes (a mother, her daughter and granddaughters in two different families). In addition, family names were almost invariably used as a first or middle name for children. Governor Buckingham's brother was Israel Matson Buckingham, after their mother, Joanna Matson. The governor's wife was Eliza Coit Ripley Buckingham; their daughter was Eliza Coit Buckingham, and her children had Buckingham as their middle names. Names and vital records information are available for many of the millionaires' children and, in some cases, grandchildren. Please visit "Norwich Millionaires' Triangle" on Facebook for more information.

As I worked on this book, a number of people helped smooth the way and were kind enough to help in my research and share their expertise. Special thanks are due to Vivian Zoe and Barry Wilson at Slater Memorial Museum; the staff at the Otis Library, especially Director Bob Farwell and reference librarian Kathy Wieland; Dianne Brown and Bill Shannon of the Norwich Historical Society; Betsey Barrett, Norwich city clerk; David Oat of the Guns of Norwich; and Paul O'Connell and Raymond H. O'Connell of Yantic Fire Engine Company No. 1.

I was privileged to meet descendants of some of the millionaires: Dianne Norman, Karen and the late Robert A. Brand, Carol Brand Connor, Joya Hoyt and Pamela Granberry. I am grateful to all of them for sharing family photos, information and stories.

I am especially grateful to Samuel H. Williamson and Lawrence H. Officer, economics professors at the University of Illinois–Chicago. Their website, Measuring Worth© (http://www.measuringworth.com), proved invaluable in my efforts to grasp the extent of the wealth of Norwich's millionaires. Amounts determined by the Measuring Worth formulas are accompanied by a copyright symbol and are used with permission.

Finally, special thanks to my family for their love, support and endless patience in listening to recitations of newly discovered facts. This book's for you.

TRICIA STALEY
Norwich, Connecticut

1
Ꞥorwich

The Rose of New England

In the center of Norwich, Connecticut, there are two streets lined with large, impressive homes on spacious lots. The streets converge into a single thoroughfare at the apex of a triangle-shaped park. More stately homes line the streets around the park.

It's almost possible to hear the *clip-clop* of hooves as a smart pair of high-stepping horses draws a carriage along the street, carrying a well-dressed manufacturer and his companion, a visitor from Boston, to the docks, where they will board the overnight steamboat for New York.

The manufacturer salutes a tall, athletic man dressed in black who is striding up Broadway. "That's Colonel Perkins," he remarks to his companion. "He's eighty-five years old and still goes to the office every day. He's been treasurer of the railroad almost forty years."

Later, as they walk toward the docks, the manufacturer stops to shake the hand of another distinguished-looking man. "Senator, good to see you. Are you heading back to Washington?" he asks.

"Yes, but I have business to attend to in New York before I travel south." The senator smiles, nods and moves off.

The manufacturer remarks, "Senator Buckingham was governor of Connecticut during the war. His family runs the Hayward Rubber Company."

This was Norwich, Connecticut, in the nineteenth century, the home of millionaire manufacturers, businessmen and important political figures. The city was known as "The Rose of New England" for its tree-lined streets and the beauty of its natural surroundings.

FOUNDED 1659
INCORPORATED 1784

NORWICH
"THE ROSE OF
NEW ENGLAND"

Norwich has been "The Rose of New England" for 150 years. *Courtesy of Bill Shannon.*

The Norwich story begins in 1659, when a group of settlers left the Saybrook colony at the mouth of the Connecticut River and traveled east on Long Island Sound until reaching the mouth of another river that the group named the Thames (rhymes with James). About twelve miles upriver, the settlers found a natural harbor at the confluence of the Thames and two other rivers and bought a nine-mile-square parcel of land from the Mohegan Indian tribe. If you imagine a letter *Y*, the Yantic River is the left arm and the Shetucket the right. The base is the Thames, which flows south to Long Island Sound. The town grew up along the riverbanks and on the plain between the arms of the *Y*.

The first settlement was established about three miles north of the harbor, where the settlers laid out farms surrounding what became the Norwich Town Green.

Throughout the eighteenth century, the importance of shipping increased, and a commercial district grew around the harbor. Maritime trade with England increased, but as Parliament imposed more taxes, Norwich, like towns in the other American colonies, began making its own goods rather than paying the ever-increasing tariffs. Mills and factories were established to provide foodstuffs and textiles.

During the Revolutionary War, its location halfway between New York and Boston put Norwich in the thick of the independence effort. Two key

This map of New London County shows the Thames River from New London north to Norwich. The Yantic River is the left fork at the top of the map, and the Shetucket to Greeneville is to the right. *Courtesy of the author.*

figures of the Revolution lived in the city. One was Samuel Huntington, a signer of the Declaration of Independence and president of the Continental Congress (1779–81) when the Articles of Confederation were adopted. The other was the brilliant general-turned-traitor Benedict Arnold, who spent his boyhood in the city.

With the end of the war, the city grew in both wealth and population. Between 1800 and 1880, Norwich's population increased sevenfold, growing about 40 percent every ten years between 1820 and 1860 and then dropping to around 20 percent growth in 1870 and 1880. Overall, the city grew from 3,476 in 1800 to 24,637 in 1900.

Early manufacturing enterprises were mainly along the Yantic River at what was called the Falls, for the nearby waterfall, located off Sachem Street just west of the parade grounds (now Chelsea Parade). A ropewalk and maritime-related ventures were established near the harbor.

The international political situation had a significant impact on Norwich development. As the colonies broke away from England, the flow of trade was diverted away from England, and Americans started to think less about importing and more about manufacturing their own goods. Before the Revolution, the town had an ironworks and factories producing linseed oil, iron wire, stockings, chocolate and paper. By 1790, there was a cotton mill, and in the early 1800s, the Goddard & Williams flour mill was also in operation at the Falls.

Domestic manufacturing became more important as the French and British fought for supremacy in Europe, and warships patrolled the West Indies and Caribbean, the destination of many Norwich ships. Shipping was largely stopped around 1807, when the Embargo Act closed ports up and down the Atlantic Coast. Quick ships with clever masters might evade the French and English warships and privateers, but it proved costly to pay the tribute money that the French, the Spanish or the pirates demanded for passage. Added to that was the threat that American seamen would be impressed into the British navy, and it was enough to make merchants and sea captains alike think twice about sea voyages.

The embargo was followed by the War of 1812, which brought more interruption of shipping. The Norwich fleet had been reduced to twenty to thirty brigs, schooners, coasting sloops or packets. Fewer than ten ship arrivals were recorded in 1811, and only three ships docked in the harbor in all of 1812. American manufacturing became even more important.

In 1813, Goddard & Williams turned to manufacturing cloth. Its mill may have been small by later standards, but it served notice on the intent to make a success of domestic textile manufacturing. About the same time, William C. Gilman established a nail-making factory that used a new invention, a machine that cut the nails more quickly and accurately than could be done by hand.

In 1823, Gilman and five investors from Boston incorporated the Thames Manufacturing Company and built a large factory at the Falls to manufacture cotton. The group included William P. Greene, who established the Thames Company in 1829, with a separate group of investors. They bought the Quinebaug Company mill on the banks of the Shetucket River, the Thames Company mill at the Falls and another mill at nearby Bozrahville. Greene bought property on Washington Street and began the Millionaires' Triangle.

The Millionaires' Triangle in Norwich. *Illustration by Sally Gonthier.*

By 1833, factories at the Falls included a large cotton mill, two paper mills, an iron foundry and a rolling mill.

One papermaking mill was run by Amos H. Hubbard, who began his operation at the Falls in 1818. His father, Thomas Hubbard, was publisher of the *Norwich Courier*. Amos had spent a few years in Java running a newspaper until the British government took over the island. He outfitted a ship with merchandise and came home to Norwich. Paper was originally made by hand, but Hubbard took advantage of the technology of the age and, in 1830, installed one of the earliest Fourdrinier machines, which mechanized the paper manufacturing process. A few years later, he and his brother, Russell, by then the publisher of the *Courier*, formed a partnership and established a second, modern paper mill in Greeneville. The partnership ended with Russell's sudden death in 1857, and not long after, Amos Hubbard sold both paper mills to Greene's Falls Company.

Later, Charles Converse constructed a building at the Falls that housed a gristmill and cork-making factory and eventually several firearms makers. The cork-making factory used a new invention by Norwich's Crocker brothers that meant hand-carved corks no longer had to be imported from Europe because they could be made more cheaply by machine in the United States.

Regular steamship service between New York and Boston also helped Norwich to prosper as a shipping center. Construction of the Norwich & Worcester Railroad in 1832–37 provided another way to move goods and people in and out of Norwich. The railroad linked with the steamship line, making it possible to travel from Boston to New York in a single day, and the trip was considered much more comfortable than making the entire journey by ship.

During the Civil War, Norwich once again rallied and saw the growth of its textile, armaments and specialty item manufacturing. Norwich gunsmiths turned out thousands of rifles every week during the war, and its textile mills produced thousands of yards of cotton and wool fabric.

After the Civil War, the federal government began collecting income taxes to retire the massive debt that financed the war. Newspapers published lists of citizens' incomes, ostensibly to ensure that everyone paid a fair share of

View overlooking the Norwich Harbor. *Courtesy of the author.*

the tax burden. The federal census in 1850, '60 and '70 included questions about the real and personal estates owned by residents. Together, the census and tax list figures provide some insight into the city's wealth—and it was impressive. MeasuringWorth.com is a website designed by two University of Illinois–Chicago professors who have developed a way to convert the value of money from one year to another. Their method, used with permission, allowed me to determine the current value of incomes and other measures of wealth ascribed to Norwich's millionaires.

In the 1860s, the average annual income was around $200. John F. Slater, by then the city's wealthiest citizen, had an annual income of $104,000 in 1865, about $18 million[©] annually in 2012. Just over $5,000 a year would be $1 million today, and Norwich had fifty-four people whose incomes topped that amount, some by a considerable amount. The 1860 census showed a number of people with real estate or personal property holdings in the six-figure range, making them multimillionaires in today's dollars.

INCOMES OF NORWICH BUSINESSMEN, 1865 AND 2012

These were considered the leading businessmen of Norwich in 1865.

Income does not include dividends from bank, insurance stock or railroad bonds. These are net amounts after taxes and interest paid by the individuals have been deducted.

LAST NAME	FIRST NAME	1865 INCOME	IN 2012 DOLLARS	OCCUPATION
Slater	John Fox	104,269	18,500,000	Textile manufacturer/ financier
Blackstone	Lorenzo	41,246	7,330,000	Textile manufacturer/ financier
Buckingham	William A.	39,968	7,110,000	Rubber goods manufacturer
Osgood	Charles	28,904	5,140,000	Wholesale drug manufacturer
Chappell	Edward	28,502	5,070,000	Lumber and coal merchant
Hubbard	Amos H.	24,082	4,280,000	Paper manufacturer
Norton	Henry B.	23,969	4,260,000	Wholesale grocer/ manufacturer
Williams	William	23,293	4,140,000	Wholesale grocer/ manufacturer
Norton	Timothy P.	22,257	3,960,000	Wholesale grocer/ manufacturer

Last Name	First Name	1865 Income	In 2012 dollars	Occupation
Sturtevant	Alfred P.	18,654	3,320,000	Hotelier/textile manufacturer
Buckingham	I.M.	17,632	3,130,000	Rubber goods manufacturer
Greene	J. Lloyd	17,600	3,130,000	Textile manufacturer
Greene	Gardiner	15,720	2,790,000	Textile manufacturer
Carew	James S.	13,827	2,460,000	Rubber goods manufacturer
Mowry	Samuel C.	12,623	2,240,000	Machinist/manufacturer
Hubbard	James L.	12,621	2,240,000	Paper manufacturer
Smith	David	12,331	2,190,000	Paper manufacturer
Ballou	Leonard	12,042	2,140,000	Textile manufacturer
Huntington	Jedidiah	11,536	2,050,000	Retired merchant
Pierce	Moses	11,126	1,980,000	Textile finishing company
Carroll	Lucius W.	11,019	1,960,000	Wholesale manufacturing supplies
Abbott	E.O.	10,080	1,790,000	Mill superintendent
Johnson	Charles	8,417	1,500,000	Banker
Foster	Lafayette	7,843	1,390,000	U.S. Senator/lawyer
Bill	Henry	6,923	1,230,000	Book publisher
Prentice	Amos W.	6,038	1,070,000	Hardware merchant
Halsey	Jeremiah	5,795	1,030,000	Lawyer
Osgood	Gilbert	5,126	911,000	Wholesale drug manufacturer
Ely	Jesse S.	5,049	898,000	Merchant/revenue assessor

Incomes from the published 1865 tax list were converted to the equivalent 2012 dollars. Note that the 1865 incomes are minimum amounts because certain dividends were excluded from taxation. *Conversions from MeasuringWorth.com.*

Norwich's manufacturing continued to grow after the war, coinciding with the pronounced growth in the national economy. Economists say the 1870s and 1880s were the period of the greatest growth in U.S. history.

Part of the growth would be attributable to the mammoth Ponemah Mill along the Shetucket River in Taftville, about three miles north of the harbor.

Towers of the Ponemah Mill rise over the mill houses of Taftville. *Courtesy of Bill Shannon.*

The mill was built in 1866–67 by Edward and Cyrus Taft. At 978 feet long and five stories high, with each floor covering an acre and a quarter, it was considered the largest cotton mill under one roof in the world.

The company was organized in 1869 as the Orrey Taft Manufacturing Company with $1.5 million in capital stock. The original shareholders included Norwich residents Lorenzo Blackstone, John F. Slater and Moses Pierce, as well as investors from Massachusetts and Rhode Island. The mill went into operation in November 1871. A second mill was constructed a few years later and a third mill in 1902. When the mill was at full capacity, about 1,500 employees produced several million yards of cotton fabric and cotton yard.

Ponemah was the first mill in the United States to import Egyptian cotton and the first manufacturer of fine cotton fabric. Up to that time, fine fabric was imported from England. One product was *soiesette*, a silky cotton used in men's furnishings and pajamas.

Another building gives strong evidence of the city's wealth at that time. Norwich City Hall is a large, ornate, imposing building that is a personification of the Gilded Age. Construction of city hall began in 1870 as Norwich's wealth was skyrocketing. The city had a bona fide millionaire in John F. Slater, with several other residents rapidly approaching millionaire status. Textile factories and firearms makers abounded, and most had done very well indeed during the Civil War.

Norwich City Hall is a fine example of Second Empire style. *Courtesy of the author.*

The new building combined the functions of a courthouse and a city hall. An act of the legislature designated Norwich the "shire town" or county seat of New London County. An earlier courthouse had been destroyed by fire. At the time, Norwich was divided into the City of Norwich (downtown and the harbor, located largely south of the current Chelsea Parade) and a separate town, called Norwich Town (the earlier settlement, north from Chelsea Parade), as well as several other villages that were eventually incorporated into the city. In 1869, the legislature authorized the city, the town and New London County to jointly construct a new building.

Today, the imposing structure at the intersection of Union Street and Broadway is the Norwich City Hall. It originally housed courts and had a police lockup in the basement, but in the twenty-first century, it holds the offices of the city government and a third-floor meeting room for the Norwich City Council.

The building, considered to be a largely untouched example of Second Empire–style architecture, was designed by Burdick & Arnold, a local architectural firm. The inside, much of which is original, has high metal ceilings, plaster ceiling medallions and original hardware. The interior finish woods are yellow pine, chestnut and black walnut. In the 1870s, the cost of construction was $350,000 (about $43.8 million© in 2012).

The structure is 100 feet long, 108 feet wide and 58 feet high with a French roof. A clock tower, added in 1909, rises 29 feet above the roof. In 1999, the city constructed a plaza in front of the building.

Despite the rapid increase in the amount of manufacturing, the center of the city remained a beautiful residential area as elaborate residences on large parcels of land were constructed along Washington Street and Broadway. Although some have been razed to allow use of the property for another purpose, a large number of original houses remain to provide a catalogue of Victorian architectural styles. The houses along the Millionaires' Triangle are considered to be among the best examples of their types in the state and include Gothic Revival, Italianate and Second Empire with its mansard roof. On many properties, the original carriage house survives, although it probably has been converted to a garage. Many of the estates had graperies and often greenhouses.

By 1870, a coachman was part of the staff at many of the houses. This was in addition to two or three maids and sometimes a cook, as well as the gardener. It becomes harder to determine the number of servants by 1880, as many apparently no longer lived in their employers' homes. The city directory listed their occupations as maid, cook, coachman or gardener but often didn't specify where or for whom they worked.

At a time when vacation was an unfamiliar concept, it was considered advantageous to have pleasant surroundings; a house near the river held the promise of a cool breeze on a hot summer day. On the west side of

Washington Street, most of the houses had grounds that extended back to the river.

The noted author and minister Henry Ward Beecher visited Norwich in 1851. Washington Street residents, he wrote, "can have the joys of the breezy wilderness at home. For, if you will go back through the garden, and then through a little pet orchard, you shall find the forest-covered bank plunging one hundred feet down toward the Yantic, and there, hidden among shrubs and wild flowers, oaks, and elms, you hear no din of wheels or clink of shops, but only the waving of leaves and the sport of birds."

Other visitors extolled the beauty of the city. An unnamed visitor wrote an article for a Rhode Island newspaper, reprinted in the *Norwich Aurora* in 1872, that described

> *the prodigality of beauty in nature and in art. I have seen much that is interesting in various towns and cities in our country recently, but nowhere such an abundance of beauty…*
>
> *Broadway and Washington streets are the two great thoroughfares running parallel from the landing* [harbor] *north, on which are most of the beautiful residences, and they are beautiful indeed, front and rear, with every adornment of the most magnificent and stately trees, most beautiful shrubbery, extensive graperies and greenhouses…*
>
> *There are a hundred homes in Norwich every one of which might be the befitting suburban residence of the most regal prince or duke of Europe. But take for instance a single neighborhood on Broadway and Washington streets embracing the houses of John F. Slater, James Hubbard, Dr. Osgood, Mayor Greene and his two brothers, Mr. Blackstone, Newton Perkins, Gen. Aiken, Leonard Ballou, Col. Converse and others, and I challenge the whole country to match it in beauty of grounds and dwellings.*

By 1850, enough wealth was concentrated in Norwich that businessmen began thinking about amenities for the town. Bigger churches, a theater and an assembly hall were among buildings constructed in the city, sometimes by an individual who perceived a need.

The most significant new venture of the decade was Norwich Free Academy (NFA). Reverend John P. Gulliver, pastor of the Broadway Congregational Church, suggested it would be desirable for all of the city's young people to be educated, not just those from wealthy families. In 1853, he approached the city's "wealthiest and noblest" men to raise $75,000 to construct a school that would educate rich and poor, boys and girls. Within two years, the school was incorporated, and the first students entered in 1856. The building was just off Broadway, opposite Williams Park (now Chelsea Parade), adjacent to the homes of Senator Lafayette Foster and Amos W. Prentice, which are now part of the NFA campus.

Life was pleasant for the families living along Washington Street and Broadway. Almost universally, they had two or three female domestic servants, probably maids and a cook. Some had coachmen, and by 1880, many had a gardener. They were religious and built their lives around family, home and church.

In the later years, the men belonged perhaps to the Rowing Club or one of the social clubs, such as the Arcanum Club on Church Street or to the Masons. They might attend performances at the Broadway Theater or hear the lecturers of the day, such as Mark Twain or Reverend Henry Ward Beecher.

Few of the men retired; most retained their business ties, at least in the census and city directory listings, until illness or death precluded such activity. Leonard Ballou declared himself a retired manufacturer, but even though he sold his mills, he devoted himself to his other interests. Colonel George Perkins remained in his post as treasurer of the Norwich & Worcester Railroad long after he passed his ninetieth birthday.

Usually, after they completed their educations, sons entered the family business. For some, like Winslow Tracy Williams, their educations were interrupted by the need for them to take over operation of the business. Wives and daughters would pay visiting calls and belong to the Ladies' Aid at their churches or United Workers, the social service agency that served the city's poor.

There were dinners in the winter and garden parties in the warmer months. Steamboats ran excursions to the seashore at New London, Westerly or Block Island. Fishing, shooting and hunting trips to Maine or perhaps the Adirondack Mountains of New York were part of the gentlemen's calendar of events.

A much-anticipated event of the spring or early summer was the Harvard-Yale Regatta. The crew race between the two Ivy League colleges occurred on the Thames River not far south of Norwich. Norwich followed the rivalry closely, and chartered boats carried two hundred or more passengers downriver to view the fiercely competitive races. Throughout the 1880s and 1890s, the National Croquet Tournament came to Norwich in August, first on courts on Cliff Street and, later, Rockwell Street. The Norwich team could boast that it won the championship in 1882 and 1886.

Another much-anticipated summer activity was the New London County Fair, which found many of the millionaires entering flowers, vegetables and animals, and their names appeared often on the prize lists. Horse racing would have brought a different kind of competition, and most of the millionaires at one time or another had a horse of which they were particularly proud, leading to spirited competition in the races.

Afternoon tea also was part of the social ritual, as well as gatherings at the private homes for dinners or birthday celebrations. As they are today, these celebrations might be planned around themes. For example, when manufacturer Leonard Ballou turned eighty, all of the guests were eighty or older.

High points of the social season were the balls that occurred for occasions like the city's bicentennial celebration in 1859 or visits by New York's Seventh Regiment in the years after the Civil War.

Election years carried their own excitement. Norwich was an important city, and local names were often on the state and federal ballots. William A. Buckingham was Connecticut's governor throughout the Civil War and then was sent to the U.S. Senate. Norwich resident Lafayette S. Foster was a senator and, as Senate president pro tempore, became acting vice president when Andrew Johnson succeeded to the presidency after the Lincoln assassination. Mayor J. Lloyd Green, Foster and others were candidates for the governor's chair. Norwich was important enough for candidates to stop in the city to speak.

Papers were full of descriptions of the "Grand Illumination"—lanterns hung to adorn houses and grounds—to mark Abraham Lincoln's election in 1860. Similar illuminations occurred for other occasions.

Presidential visits and occasions that drew famous visitors occurred with some regularity. Weddings would most likely be elaborate events that might include not only friends and neighbors but also distinguished visitors. Sometimes, well-known visitors were attending events such as a city anniversary or Independence Day celebration; other times, the occasion was the funeral of one of the city's luminaries, such as Senator and former governor William Buckingham, Senator Lafayette Foster, John Slater or Colonel George L. Perkins. Former president Rutherford B. Hayes was among mourners at John F. Slater's funeral in 1884. Andrew Carnegie and famed sculptor Augustus Saint-Gaudens were among a group from the Metropolitan Museum in New York that visited to see the cast gallery at Slater Museum and dine at the home of William and Ellen Slater. In 1909, President William Howard Taft

Scenes at the 250th Anniversary of the Settlement of the Town of Norwich.

1909

The Pageant—View of Colonial Minuet

The Pageant—Mohegan Tribe of Indians

No. 1

No. 2—Line of March passing Wauregan House Corner—No. 3

No. 4

Winslow T. Williams

William H. Taft

Mayor Lippitt

Founder's Monument

City Hall

D.A.R. Memorial Fountain

Chelsea Parade—View of Memorial to Founders.

This photo collage commemorates the city's 1909 Quarter Millenium Celebration. *Courtesy of Yantic Fire Engine Company No. 1.*

was a guest at the Norwich Quarter Millennium Celebration, the city's 250th birthday.

Many of the millionaires' houses remain to provide some insights into the people who lived there and their lives. Their stories are not presented in any particular order after the Slaters, Blackstones, Buckinghams and Senator Foster, the most prominent among the city's residents.

2

THE SLATERS

The Slaters were the wealthiest family in Norwich, and by 1870, John Slater was a millionaire. His annual income in 1865 was $104,000 ($18 million© in 2012), more than twice what anyone else made. Their wealth didn't spare the Slaters from life's sorrows. Four of their six children died in childhood, and their surviving daughter died as a young mother. Slater married Marianna Hubbard, the girl next door, but after thirty years, they separated. Although they remained married, they lived apart for the last years of their lives. John Slater was awarded the Congressional Medal of Honor for his million-dollar John F. Slater Fund for the Education of Freedmen.

JOHN FOX SLATER (1815–1884)

Main Street/228 Broadway

John Fox Slater may have been destined to be a textile manufacturer because of his family background, but he gained widespread national attention as a major philanthropist. In 1882, he put up $1 million to provide education for former slaves, and the John F. Slater Fund for the Education of Freedmen set a high standard for later philanthropists.

Congressional Medal of Honor recipient John Fox Slater. *Courtesy of Slater Memorial Museum.*

J.F. Slater was born into the manufacturing dynasty begun by his great-uncle Samuel, the "Father of the American Industrial Revolution," who brought textile mill technology to Rhode Island. Young John was born in 1815, the son of John and Ruth (Bucklin) Slater in Slatersville (now North Smithfield), Rhode Island, the seat of the family's manufacturing enterprises.

Like other youths of his time, Slater was educated at academies in Massachusetts and Plainfield Academy in Connecticut. At seventeen, he joined the family textile firm, and by the time he was twenty-one, he was overseeing the mill in Hopeville, Connecticut.

In 1842, Slater moved to the house best known as the former Elks Home on Main Street in Norwich, and in 1844, he married Marianna Hubbard, whose family lived next door.

Slater moved his family to a mansion at Broadway and Broad Street in 1861. Originally built by Charles Rockwell, the eight-acre parcel was bounded by Broad Street, Slater Avenue, Cedar Street and Broadway. Slater paid Captain James L. Day $50,000 for the house and grounds.

The 1870 census showed Slater to be a very wealthy man. At age fifty-five, he was a true millionaire, with assets of $1,768,000, about $442 million© in 2012. At that time, he was actually much wealthier than John D. Rockefeller, who was just starting Standard Oil in Ohio and reported only $335,000 in total holdings. The household included his wife and son, three servants and a coachman.

Slater was president of the group involved in the restructuring of the Orrey Taft mill in Norwich's Taftville section, which became the fabulously successful Ponemah Mill about 1870. His other manufacturing interests included mills in Lawrence and Worcester, Massachusetts, and Providence, Rhode Island, and the Slater mills in Connecticut that were his share of the family business.

Slater's interests included railroads, and he was a director of the Chicago & Alton and the Norwich & Worcester Railroads. He was also a director of several local banks and the Norwich Fire Insurance Co.

Slater was one of the original incorporators of Norwich Free Academy and donated more than $15,000, including funds to outfit the school. In addition to unpublicized gifts in Norwich, Slater endowed Park Congregational Church and provided funds for its maintenance, and with Lafayette Foster, he provided a building for United Workers, a social services agency in Norwich. He also funded construction of the Slater Library in Jewett City.

In the 1880 census, Slater was sixty-eight years of age and lived at the mansion with three servants and his son, William, twenty-two, a student.

Establishment of the Slater Fund in 1882 catapulted Slater to national prominence as a philanthropist. It would be another decade before Carnegie, Rockefeller, Vanderbilt and others began their major philanthropies. At the time, Slater's million-dollar fund ($216,000,000© in 2012) was an unimaginable sum.

He chose as chairman of the fund trustees Rutherford B. Hayes, who had just completed his term as U.S. president. The original board also included Slater's son, William; Norwich native Daniel Coit Gilman, president of Johns Hopkins University; William Dodge of Waterbury, the "Dodge" of the Phelps-Dodge Corporation; and Lyme, Connecticut native Morrison R. Waite, chief justice of the U.S. Supreme Court. In 1883, Slater was awarded the Congressional Medal of Honor, the nation's highest civilian award, for his contribution to the betterment of the formerly enslaved.

Institutions that benefitted from the Slater Fund included the Hampton Institute (Virginia), Tuskegee Institute (Alabama), Spelman Seminary (Atlanta) and Fiske University (Nashville). The Slater Fund was later consolidated into the Southern Education Foundation.

Early in 1884, newspapers reported Slater was the victim of a mysterious illness that didn't allow him to eat or digest food. There was at least one trip to New York for consultation with eminent doctors. When John F. Slater died on May 7, 1884, obituaries appeared in newspapers across the county, hailing him as founder of the Slater Fund. One report, however, noted that when the fund was established, a factory hand suggested that if Slater were interested in "ameliorating the 'condition of the poor laboring classes, he could have found a rich field directly in his own mills.'"

Slater's public funeral was at Park Congregational Church in Norwich after a private service at the mansion. The bearers were not prominent men, but rather the mill superintendents and overseers of various departments, some of whom had worked for Slater for more than thirty years. Former president Hayes and other members of the Slater Fund board were among the mourners.

A memorial volume commissioned by William Slater contained a brief biography of his father and the text of the funeral sermon preached by Reverend William Howe. More than half of the volume was devoted to the Slater Fund. It lacked the tributes from municipal leaders and colleagues that were common in other memorials of the era. Whether this underscored Slater's detachment from the community around him or reflected a modesty and wished-for privacy cannot be determined.

Within a week after his death, the newspapers were speculating about the disposition of the Slater estate, estimated at $20 million. One report called the community "agog" over provisions of the will, which supposedly included the funds to build a hospital and an opera house and create a public park and gardens on the estate grounds. When the will was finally proved, there were no public bequests; the fortune stayed within the family, with bequests to son-in-law Francis Bartlett and his surviving daughter and the remainder to son William.

Within a few years, however, the city had ample benefit from the Slater fortune as William Slater provided major financing for a local hospital and, in memory of his father, established the Slater Memorial Museum.

MARIANNA HUBBARD SLATER (1824–1889)

76/276 Broadway

Marianna Hubbard Slater seemed to have a charmed life. Her father was a wealthy manufacturer; her ancestors were the wealthy and influential and included senators and governors. She married the boy next door who became the richest man in town. She also suffered what was, perhaps, more than a fair share of life's sorrows.

She was born on February 15, 1824, to Amos Hallam and Eliza (Lanman) Hubbard, one of the city's wealthiest couples. Amos and his brother, Russell (publisher of the *Norwich Courier*), were partners in a paper-manufacturing mill. Her mother was one of the twelve children of James and Marian Griswold (Chandler) Lanman. James Lanman, a U.S. senator from 1819 to 1825, was a cousin of Presidents John Adams and John Quincy Adams.

In the mid-1870s, Mariana Hubbard Slater moved to this house at 276 Broadway. It was later occupied by industrialist Moses Pierce. *Courtesy of Slater Memorial Museum.*

Eliza's sister Joanna Boylston Lanman was the first wife of Senator Lafayette Foster of Norwich. The Hubbards lived on Main Street where the Norwich Post Office building now stands.

Marianna Hubbard was just twenty on May 13, 1844, when she married John F. Slater, nine years her senior. Over the next thirteen years, she bore him six children, but only Marianna and William—the eldest and the youngest—survived to adulthood.

Eight years after the Slaters moved to their Broadway estate, the mansion was the site of daughter Marianna's wedding to Boston attorney Francis C. Bartlett on March 31, 1869.

By 1876, Mrs. Slater was living at 76 Broadway with a complete household staff including a cook, maid and a coachman. The house is now the residence of the Roman Catholic bishop of Norwich. Financing her establishment probably wasn't a problem, as she had inherited $60,000 ($10.7 million©) when her father died in 1865, and Slater reportedly provided $10,000 ($2.86 million©) annually for her living expenses.

Little is known about Mrs. Slater's life, but she apparently kept in touch with her extended family. In the 1880 census, enumerated in her household was twenty-two-year-old James Penniman, identified as an adopted son. He was the son of her cousin James Penniman, whose parents were her Aunt Marian (Lanman) and Uncle Obediah Penniman. Young James became Dr. James Hosmer Penniman, who later became a well-known author, educator and authority on George Washington. His brother, Josiah, was provost and president of the University of Pennsylvania.

Marianna Slater died of pneumonia on February 19, 1889. Her will included a $10,000 bequest to the Norwich Free Academy reserve fund. Despite the separation, much note was taken of her status as the widow of the founder of the $1 million Slater Fund, and death notices appeared in newspapers across the nation.

WILLIAM A. SLATER (1857–1919)

228 Broadway

He was "Bert" to his classmates at Harvard and "Will" in later life, and although he was the son of a very wealthy man, William Alfred Slater had a "remarkable sweetness of nature…he was always doing kindnesses," said the obituary in a Harvard College class report.

William A. Slater was born in Norwich on December 25, 1857. Little is known about his early years, except that he went to Europe about 1875 for two years of study before entering Harvard, where he was in the class behind Theodore Roosevelt. The periodic Harvard Class reports provide some insight into the activities of Slater's later years.

Left: William A. Slater. *Courtesy of Slater Memorial Museum. Right*: Ellen Peck Slater. *Courtesy of Slater Memorial Museum.*

Although he didn't play any major sports, Slater was considered "a pleasant companion" at Harvard and was well liked enough to be First Man on the First Ten of the Dicky. In Harvard-speak, that means he was the first man in his class chosen for the DKE, a secret club whose members are chosen in groups of ten, with each group choosing the succeeding ten. Membership was considered a high honor tinged with notoriety, apparently for the last stage of the initiation, which reportedly involved being burned on the arm six times with a lighted cigar. Slater apparently was unaffected by the attention that came with DKE membership and remained "simply the quiet, unaffected, kindly gentleman he had always been."

Slater also belonged to Hasty Pudding, the art club, and several extracurricular groups.

After graduation in 1881, Slater returned to Norwich and embarked on the training course his father arranged in management of the mills. He also took his place as a trustee of the million-dollar Slater Fund with well-known men twice his age. After J.F. Slater died, Will succeeded him as president of the Ponemah Mill and as a director of the Chicago & Alton Railroad. He was, as well, a trustee of Norwich Free Academy.

Will Slater's marriage to Ellen Burnett Peck in 1885 was apparently a small ceremony at her mother's home in Norwich. The local newspaper carried only a brief notice of the marriage, which apparently was kept low key because his father had died only a year before. In a later class report, Slater said he was in Europe from June 1885 to June 1886, suggesting the couple took a European wedding trip.

Before they left, Slater had begun work on two memorials to his father: a written memorial booklet and an art museum on the grounds of Norwich Free Academy. Both were completed after the return to Norwich, and the Slater Memorial Museum opened to much fanfare in 1888.

In 1892, after a six-month Mediterranean cruise aboard his yacht *Sagamore*, Will Slater commissioned the Bath Iron Works in Maine to build a new 231-foot yacht to be called *Eleanor* after his daughter. The yacht was equipped with two electric power plants, a desalinization plant to provide water, a steam laundry with separate drying room, a spacious and fully equipped kitchen and berths for crew and servants. Newspaper descriptions marveled that all rooms had hot/cold and fresh/salt running water. Rooms were paneled in various woods, and the main saloon was hung with paintings worth an estimated $60,000. The captain's dining room by itself measured 12 by 16 feet.

The Slaters and their children, Eleanor and William A. Jr., took an around-the-world cruise aboard *Eleanor* from October 1894 to November 1895, returning overland to Connecticut from California.

Back in Norwich, in 1895, Slater offered the city $10,000 ($1.2 million© in 2012) toward the establishment of a normal school for the training of teachers with an endowment that would produce $7,000 a year. He withdrew the offer early in 1896 because of what was described as the antagonistic attitude of board of education members. The plan ignited considerable public controversy over removal of property from the tax rolls. He also contributed $350,000 (more than $45 million© in 2012) to establish a hospital, which was named for the recently deceased William W. Backus, whose contribution was far less than Slater's. Newspapers speculated that was the last straw for Slater, who was offended by the city's failure to properly appreciate his gifts.

The family left Norwich in April 1896 and lived in France for about seven years. The estate on Broadway was sold at least twice before the mansion was razed and the land divided into individual building lots.

In the early 1900s, Slater had begun suffering from an unnamed painful disease that ultimately incapacitated him. As his mobility deteriorated, he turned to reading and the study of art. In 1905, he coauthored the book *Paintings of the Louvre, Italian and Spanish*.

In 1907, the Slaters established their main residence in Washington, D.C., with seasonal homes in Beverly and Lenox, Massachusetts.

In Washington during the social season, the Slater name regularly appeared among the high-powered and socially prominent Washingtonians attending receptions at the White House and dinners for high-ranking visitors. They also took an active role in functions for charitable causes, such as the Red Cross.

His mother's death left Will Slater the last of his immediate family, but it appears that Slater was close to his in-laws. When Ellen's sister May Peck married Charles Turnbull of Boston, Will reportedly presented them with a check for $100,000; Ellen's gift was a house on Beacon Street. Visits from her sisters were noted in the newspapers, and the list of guests at the launch of the *Eleanor* included Ellen's mother and sisters and their husbands, as well as Will's brother-in-law, Francis Bartlett, and niece Caroline and her husband, H.K. Sears. Bartlett was a passenger aboard the yacht for part of the *Eleanor*'s long voyage.

Slater designated his Peck brothers-in-law, Joseph Ely and Charles Turnbull, both of whom were attorneys, to handle his legal affairs in Providence and Boston, respectively. He also involved them in management of the mills. Both died before he did, but there were bequests in the Slater will to the Peck sisters-in-law in recognition of the service provided by their husbands.

Slater was a member of a social club in Boston, five more in New York and three in Washington. By the time he died on February 25, 1919, he was better known as a "noted clubman" than as a manufacturer or philanthropist in some obituaries.

Ellen Peck Slater died on November 27, 1941, in Santa Barbara, California, where she moved in the late 1920s, apparently to be near her son and his wife.

3

THE BLACKSTONES

LORENZO BLACKSTONE (1819–1888)
58/138 Washington Street

When Lorenzo Blackstone came to Norwich in 1857, he had already made a fortune in rubber goods by introducing rubber overshoes from the Goodyear Company to England, which extended his business throughout England and the Continent. Eventually, Blackstone began to sell products from the Hayward Rubber Company of Colchester, Connecticut, which brought in several hundred thousand dollars annually. His business dealings with Hayward Rubber prompted him to become an investor in the firm.

Lorenzo Blackstone was born in 1819 in Branford, Connecticut. He numbered among his forebears the earliest settlers of Boston and William Blackstone, the famed jurist. He married Emily Norton in 1842 and went to England, where their three eldest children were born.

By 1855, Blackstone had returned to America, while continuing to run his business abroad. Through the Buckingham brothers at Hayward Rubber and his Norton brothers-in-law, Blackstone was introduced to Norwich and found the city a desirable place to relocate his family.

The Blackstones' home in Norwich was an Italianate villa at 138 Washington Street. Old maps indicate that there was a wing on each side of the structure that remains today.

Above: The Lorenzo Blackstone residence at 138 Washington Street was originally much larger with a wing on each side of the main house, which survives. *Photo by the author.*

Left: Industrialist Lorenzo Blackstone. *Courtesy of the author.*

Although he already had a fortune, Blackstone became a manufacturer. In 1859, Blackstone and the Norton brothers secured the rights to a property where a mill had burned down. Within a few years, they acquired three other mill properties and built modern facilities at each site. The firm also owned the Potokett (later named Totokett) Mill in Norwich and the Pequot Mill in nearby Montville and, around 1860, acquired mills in Killingly from Leonard Ballou.

By the 1870 census, the Blackstones and their five children lived with three servants. Blackstone's holdings totaled an $850,000 personal estate (about $224 million© in 2012). His twenty-three-year-old son, DeTrafford, a bookkeeper, had $6,200 ($1.6 million©) of his own.

With John F. Slater and others, Blackstone became a member of the executive committee that reorganized the Ponemah Mill in Taftville and brought the cotton mill operation to financial success.

Blackstone was an original incorporator and trustee of Norwich Free Academy. In addition, he was an original trustee and first president of the Chelsea Bank and director of the Thames National Bank. During the 1870s, he served two terms as mayor of Norwich and later was a state representative and state senator.

He also had deep connections with a number of railroads in the West. He was a director of the Chicago & Alton Railroad, whose president was his brother, Timothy Beach Blackstone. The Blackstones' sister, Ellen, married Henry B. Plant, who built railroads in Florida. Their son, Morton Freeman Plant, built Branford House (on the campus of the University of Connecticut–Avery Point in Groton) and was a major benefactor of the then Connecticut College for Women.

After they married, most of the Blackstone children lived near their parents. DeTrafford lived on Broadway near St. Patrick's Church. Ella and her husband, Frederick Jabez Huntington, lived in Boston and New York for many years but returned to Norwich by the 1900 census, when they were enumerated with his mother at 197 Broadway. Harriet and Fred Camp lived on Washington Street, two doors down from her parents. William and his bride, Julia Squires of Brooklyn, New York, lived with his parents for about five years before moving to their 206 Washington Street home. Louis married Grace Webb and lived nearby on Broad Street with his wife and daughter.

After her husband's death in 1888, Emily Blackstone continued to live at 138 Washington Street until her death twelve years later.

Lorenzo Blackstone's estate was estimated at $1.6 million ($348 million© in 2012). Division of its shares was the subject of a lawsuit by DeTrafford because he was given only life use of most of his share. A later suit that reached the Connecticut Supreme Court centered on disposition of trust fund monies after the death of Blackstone children without issue.

JAMES DETRAFFORD BLACKSTONE (1846–1898)

55/219 Broadway

The house at 219 Broadway was the scene of some of the city's most widely publicized scandals of the 1880s. They included divorce, kidnapping, reconciliation and a fight over an estate that pitted son against mother.

The owner was James DeTrafford Blackstone, the Blackstones' eldest son. Born in England in 1847, he graduated from Yale's Scientific School in 1868. His classmates called him "Traf," apparently because he used DeTrafford as his given name.

After graduation, he returned to Norwich and assumed a place in running the Totokett and Pequot Mills. He also was secretary-treasurer of

The home of DeTrafford Backstone at 219 Broadway was the scene of a much-publicized kidnapping. *Photo by the author.*

the Occum Water Power Company and a member of the Norwich Board of Trade. He was regarded as a good and public-spirited businessman.

In 1875, he surprised the city by appearing with a wife, Lillie Whittaker, whom he apparently married on a trip to New York City. It was said that Traf Blackstone had sown considerable wild oats, and although at thirty he was considered settled and a "polished gentleman," he was still "a man of the world" who was fond of fast horses.

His wife's antecedents were described as "peculiar"—she was variously said to be the niece of a hotel proprietor, mistress of a New York merchant or an actress appearing in a New York show. Nevertheless, she was a beautiful blonde, charming enough so that with the Blackstone name, she was accepted into local society. Her position was cemented with an appearance as the heroine in a home talent operetta produced for charity by the city's elite.

Their only child was born in 1876, a son called Lorenzo after his grandfather and nicknamed "Rennie." Around Christmas 1877, Lillie Blackstone left town, supposedly for a visit, but rumors of a separation were confirmed a short time later when she filed for divorce on the grounds of cruelty. The child remained with Traf, but it was unclear whether there was any definite award of custody.

In October 1878, DeTrafford Blackstone and his father were away on a business trip when Lillie, accompanied by her stepfather and two men, went to her former home and asked for little Rennie. News reports at the time said the mother had previously been allowed to see the child, so the nursemaid didn't object when Lillie asked to hold him. Once she had the child, Mrs. Blackstone and her companions drove off in a carriage.

The nursemaid notified DeTrafford's brother William and Uncle Henry Norton, who were attending a wedding reception. She also sent for the police, and an officer was dispatched to delay departure of the 4:30 p.m. train. Much confusion apparently ensued as police were reluctant to forcibly detain a lady, and legal minds contemplated action such as a writ of habeas corpus.

When Mrs. Blackstone and the child were finally brought back to Norwich, the city attorney and the Blackstones' lawyer were agreed they had no grounds to hold her. She and her companions left in a carriage headed toward Westerly, Rhode Island, to escape Connecticut's legal jurisdiction. One newspaper article suggested the popular belief that she wanted the child not for love, but rather for the money she could get for his return. Traf later located Rennie in a New York convent school and brought him back to Norwich. Some arrangement must have been reached, for young Lorenzo was enumerated with his father and servants, including a nurse, in the 1880 census.

Three years after the kidnapping, Lillie Blackstone was again at the heart of a widely reported newspaper scandal. In November 1879, she married Samuel Sondheim, a handsome, wealthy twenty-nine-year-old cotton broker four years her elder. His family objected because of her background, but after examining her character, their rabbi was unable to find any reason to deny her conversion to the Jewish faith. Sondheim installed his new wife in a home in Yonkers and indulged her extravagances. In fall 1880, she took a solo four-month trip to Europe, as business kept her husband from going with her. When she returned, he greeted her with a $1,000 bracelet as a welcoming gift.

Two weeks after her return, they were to attend a welcome-home dinner at his parents' home. Mrs. Sondheim failed to appear, and a search determined that she had left her husband for a man she met on the return voyage. She took with her the bracelet and a $1,000 check from her husband for housekeeping money.

Meanwhile, in 1881, Traf Blackstone married Annie Sybil Rich, and the marriage lasted until her death in 1894. By then, Rennie was a student at Yale. His mother had been living abroad for about fifteen years, to develop her significant artistic talent. Claiming that she missed her son, she returned to the United States and visited him at Yale.

Rennie had apparently never stopped hoping his parents would reconcile, so he praised each of them to the other. His efforts bore fruit, and Traf and his former wife, by then called Sarah or Sadie, remarried on February 24, 1897. Traf installed a studio in their Broadway home so she could pursue her art. Their newfound happiness lasted just over a year before the paralysis that Traf had suffered for the previous five years claimed his life on March 7, 1898.

As DeTrafford Blackstone's estate was being settled, it became obvious he had for years been living beyond his means. He'd been given life use—rather than outright inheritance—of his share of his father's estate, which instead was left to young Lorenzo, who was named executor with absolute control of the estate. This led to yet another round of public altercation for Sadie Blackstone, who had reportedly become estranged from her son over his choice of wife, apparently disapproving of Annie Carruthers, daughter of the Norwich postmaster.

Young Lorenzo pledged to settle his father's debts from his own funds and offered a "dividend" to the creditors, many of whom preferred that to the smaller amount that would come from probate. His mother, however, refused the twenty-five-dollar weekly stipend he offered. She petitioned the court for seventy-five dollars weekly to match the allowance her husband had provided. She remained in New York, and it was said she unsuccessfully brought action against the estate because she did not want the house in her daughter-in-law's hands.

WILLIAM NORTON BLACKSTONE (1853–1907)

206 Washington Street

If his brother DeTrafford was the black sheep, William Norton Blackstone was the good son. By all appearances, he lived a quiet life and was "universally esteemed for a business life above reproach."

William was born in Norwich on September 1, 1853. Little information is known about his life, but he apparently joined the family business about 1875.

He married Julia F. Squires in New York on June 13, 1883, in a ceremony performed by William's cousin Reverend Frank L. Norton (son of his uncle

The William Blackstone residence at 206 Washington Street is now the site of the Blackstone Apartments. *Courtesy of Bill Shannon.*

Timothy Norton). Attendants included William's brother Louis, Norwich friends Will Slater and Will Mowry and Ella Norton, another cousin. The guest list included a number of Norwich names, as well as William's uncle Henry and aunt Ellen Plant.

For about five years, the young Blackstones lived with his parents and then moved to the Italianate villa at 206 Washington Street, the site now occupied by the Blackstone Apartments. Ownership concerns were raised in 1907 when members of the Mohegan Indian tribe claimed the houses in that area were built on a royal burial ground adjacent to the grave of the great tribal Chief Uncas. But the issue was resolved, and the landowners stayed.

Little is known of the couple's activities, although their presence at Long Branch, New Jersey, a beach resort popular with many U.S. presidents of the era, was recorded in an 1885 newspaper article.

In 1884, William was the agent for the Pequot mill and apparently was promoted, as a year later, he was agent for the much larger Attawaugan Company. After his father's death, William filled his father's seat on the board of the Chicago & Alton Railroad.

He was also vice-president of the Thames National Bank, a director of the Chelsea Savings Bank and president of the Uncas National Bank and became a director of the Bulletin Company in 1898. He eventually became treasurer of both the Attawaugan and Pequot parent companies.

When his uncle Timothy Blackstone died in 1900, William received a $250,000 bequest ($47.4 million©).

William's death on August 3, 1907, left Julia a childless widow. Although she didn't remarry, census entries show an adopted daughter, whose name was variously given as Jeanette or Janet. Janet Vaughn and her husband were still living with Julia at 206 Washington Street in the 1940 census. Julia died in 1941.

Frederick Sewall Camp (1848-1907)

54/124 Washington Street

Frederick Sewall Camp came to Norwich in about 1871. He was born on September 30, 1848, near Watertown, New York, the son of Ann Elizabeth (Sewall) and Talcott Hale Camp, a Watertown bank president.

Camp worked as a clerk at the Ponemah Mill, and in October 1874, he married Harriet Bell Blackstone, daughter of one of the mill owners.

Frederick S. Camp's family occupied this house at 124 Washington Street. *Photo by the author.*

Newspaper reports describe the wedding as a "fashionable affair" attended by many prominent citizens. The Camps were the parents of four children.

In 1875, the Camps were part of Lorenzo Blackstone's household, but by 1880, they were in their own home at 54 Washington Street. In the 1880 census, Frederick Camp was identified as a manufacturer.

On January 2, 1907, the *Washington Post* reported Camp's death by his own hand, noting he had been despondent and ill with Bright's disease for a half year. After her husband's death, Harriet Camp moved to 280 Broadway, where she remained until her death.

4

The Buckinghams, the Aikens and the Carews

William A. Buckingham and his youngest brother, Israel Matson, were born in Lebanon, the sons of Samuel and Joanna (Matson) Buckingham.

They started their business careers as merchants, but after William became an investor in the Hayward Rubber Company in Colchester, that became their sole business endeavor and made them wealthy men. After William became governor of Connecticut, his brother Israel continued running Hayward Rubber.

William Alfred Buckingham (1804–1875)

40/307 Main Street

William A. Buckingham's six years as a U.S. senator are often overshadowed by his efforts on behalf of the state and the Union during the Civil War. Buckingham was governor from 1858 to 1866, an unheard of eight one-year terms.

Buckingham was born on May 28, 1804, and educated at the local schools and Bacon Academy in nearby Colchester. He came to Norwich to work in his uncle Giles Buckingham's dry goods store and then worked in New York City before returning to Norwich in 1826 to open a dry goods store.

Above: William A. Buckingham's residence at 307 Main Street is now the city-owned Buckingham Memorial. *Courtesy of the author.*

Left: Governor and Senator William A. Buckingham. *Courtesy of Slater Memorial Museum.*

On September 27, 1830, he married Eliza Coit Ripley and had two children. His son died at an early age.

For a while, Buckingham manufactured carpets, but by 1848, his main focus was the Hayward Rubber Company in Colchester, although he remained a stockholder in other manufacturing enterprises. Hayward Rubber was founded by Nathaniel Hayward, who, with Charles Goodyear, was involved in the invention of vulcanized rubber in 1838. Buckingham invested in the venture and became manager and treasurer of the company.

Buckingham was elected to four one-year terms as mayor of Norwich between 1849 and 1857. He became Connecticut's governor in 1858, the first time as a compromise candidate and then reelected an unheard of seven more times to make him one of only four Union governors to serve throughout the war. His unceasing efforts on behalf of the war effort earned him the sobriquet "Connecticut's War Governor."

Buckingham befriended Abraham Lincoln during Lincoln's New England speaking tour in 1859 and became a staunch supporter. When the war began in 1861, Governor Buckingham immediately called for seventy-five thousand enlistments and sent an aide to Washington to assure the president that help—in the form of Connecticut soldiers—was on its way to Washington. The legislature was not in session, but Buckingham secured funds from several banks to equip the troops, using his personal credit to secure the notes. For the duration of the war, Governor Buckingham declined his salary and met expenses from his personal funds as he worked tirelessly to support the Union cause.

Buckingham was an organizer of the Broadway Congregational Church when it was formed in 1840. He and Eliza purchased the organ for the new church and later financed construction of a mission chapel. He was a deacon and taught Sunday school for forty years. Much of his charity was kept private, but it is known that Yale College and its divinity school were beneficiaries of his generosity. In addition, Buckingham was among the original incorporators of the Norwich Free Academy and president of the state Temperance Union.

After the war, the governor refused another term, returned to Norwich and resumed overseeing his business interests. By the time of his wife's death in 1868, his daughter, Eliza, had married the governor's military aide General William Aiken and moved to Washington Street. The governor remained in the Main Street home he had shared with his wife for nearly thirty-seven years. She had been, he said, "the light and life of my dwelling."

Perhaps his loneliness was a factor in his willingness to accept, but in 1869, Buckingham was elected to the U.S. Senate. In Washington, he was chairman of the Indian Affairs Committee and of a committee to investigate custom house fraud.

In the 1870 census, despite being a senator, Buckingham's occupation was listed as rubber manufacturer. His household included thirty-one-year-old Elizabeth Ripley, apparently a niece who was his ward; three servants; and a coachman.

William Buckingham died on February 5, 1875. The day of his funeral, city businesses closed out of respect, and more than two thousand people waited outside in bitter zero-degree cold to pay their respects. Colleagues from Hartford and Washington and a faculty delegation from Yale attended, but the real tribute came from the people who lined the street to the church so closely that the funeral procession could barely get through. His wartime aides served as a guard of honor for the casket, but that was the extent of military pomp and ceremony. The pallbearers were the Norwich men who had been Buckingham's neighbors and friends for many years.

The Main Street house that served as an alternate state capitol during the long war years became the home of Sedgwick Post GAR. More recently, it has housed a shelter for the homeless, the city historian's office and the Norwich Historical Society.

ISRAEL MATSON BUCKINGHAM (1817–1876)

53/103 Washington Street

It could be fairly said that Israel Matson Buckingham was overshadowed by his famous elder brother. Apparently, however, I.M. Buckingham had no interest in political office; rather, he found his contentment in his home, his family and his work.

I.M. Buckingham was born on May 5, 1816, in Lebanon, Connecticut. He taught school for a time and then came to Norwich to work in his brother's dry goods store, where he gained a reputation as a good businessman. After a few years as dry goods merchants, the Buckingham brothers and James S. Carew were involved in Hayward Rubber Company, a venture so successful that all became very wealthy men.

A contemporary biographer cited I.M. Buckingham's "superior judgment...business ability...and integrity" to explain his business success and praised his lack of political ambition, enjoyment of his home and making it beautiful and devotion to friends.

Although he eschewed politics, Buckingham was active in civic affairs. Like his brother, I.M. Buckingham was an original incorporator of Norwich Free Academy. He also was a director of Chelsea Savings Bank and Thames National Bank.

It was I.M. Buckingham who, at his own expense, had printed and distributed the plan devised by David A. Wells to finance the Civil War. When it reached President Lincoln, Wells was given a major role in U.S. tax policy. Wells later became a resident of Norwich.

In 1840, I.M. Buckingham married Lydia Carew—sister of James S. Carew, the Buckingham brothers' business partner—and had three children.

Although he built a substantial fortune, when the census-taker came calling, I.M. Buckingham consistently gave his occupation as "bookkeeper." Between 1850 and 1870, the family consistently had two to four servants. Other family members were also included in the household. James Carew was living with them in 1850. By 1870, son William; his wife, Mary; and their infant daughter were living with the Buckinghams.

The November 18, 1868 marriage of William A. Buckingham II and Mary Day Reynolds was the event of the season in Norwich and received elaborate newspaper coverage. The 8:00 p.m. ceremony at Christ Episcopal Church was followed by an 8:30 to midnight reception at the bride's family home Ridge Hill, the old L'Hommidieu/Reynolds estate on the site of what is now the William W. Backus Hospital.

Mary Day Reynolds was the daughter of the well-known mariner Captain Charles L. and Helen (Downing) Reynolds. Mary Day was escorted by her guardian, Captain James L. Day, another wealthy mariner. The guest list included such illustrious names as Slater, Blackstone, Foster, Greene, Law and Webster (Mary's brother married Daniel Webster's granddaughter). The young Buckinghams were the parents of five children.

After Israel Buckingham's death on May 25, 1876, Lydia stayed on with William, Mary, their children, three servants and a gardener. Lydia continued to live with her son and his family until her death in 1901.

GENERAL WILLIAM APPLETON AIKEN (1833–1929)

65/157 Washington Street

William A. Aiken was Governor Buckingham's chief aide during the Civil War and later became a prominent businessman in Norwich.

He was born on April 18, 1833, in Manchester, Vermont, the son of John Aiken and his second wife, Mary Means Appleton, whose father was president of Bowdoin College and sister Jane was the wife of President Franklin Pierce. John Aiken was an educator, then mill agent and treasurer in Lowell, Massachusetts, and New Hampshire. He was president of the trustees of Andover Phillips Academy.

William Aiken attended public and private schools and spent the two years before the war as a grocer in Chicago. When the war broke out, he enlisted in the navy, where he was acting assistant paymaster. He saw action in the Battle of Port Royal near Hilton Head, South Carolina.

General William and Eliza (Buckingham) Aiken and their family lived in this Greek Revival house at 157 Washington Street. *Photo by the author.*

In 1862, Governor Buckingham appointed Aiken quartermaster general of Connecticut with the rank of brigadier general. As a staff aide, Aiken had successfully completed a mission on April 22, 1861, to deliver dispatches from Buckingham to President Lincoln. In the early days of the war, Washington was surrounded by Southern states and Maryland, which was filled with Southern sympathizers. Aiken traveled by train to Pennsylvania and then by skiff and covered wagon to Baltimore, where he found the streets "full of people, some of them in uniforms, and most of them wearing rebel badges" and quickly concluded that "no man could avow Unionism there, and preserve his life in safety for a moment."

A fellow traveler secured travel passes, and they paid fifty dollars for a carriage to take them to Washington, where Aiken met with General Winfield Scott, whose response to the dispatches underscored the seriousness of the situation—no intelligence about troop movement had been available for three days. The next morning, Aiken met with President Lincoln, who was distressed about being cut off from the rest of the Union. News of Connecticut's support and the expected arrival of Northern troops cheered and relieved the president, Aiken said.

On August 28, 1861, William Aiken married Eliza Coit Buckingham, the only child of the governor and his wife, and had seven children.

When General Aiken returned to Norwich after the war, he worked at two companies and then became owner and president of Norwich Nickel and Brass Company.

In the 1870 census, the Aikens and four of their children lived with four servants at 65 Washington Street. The general, whose occupation was lock manufacturer, was listed with $20,000 real estate and $3,000 personal estate (a total of over $6 million©). By the 1880 census, three more children were listed. Although the census contains no information about their holdings, they were undoubtedly well off with Eliza's inheritance after her father's death in 1875 in addition to the general's earnings from a successful factory.

The general was active in civic affairs and served as the first president of the Norwich Board of Trade. He also was chairman of the trustees of Otis Library for twenty-five years. He belonged to many other organizations, including the Connecticut Civil Service Reform Association, and served on government reform commissions.

General Aiken died in 1929 at the age of ninety-six, and Eliza Aiken died in 1933 at age ninety-five.

Their daughter Eliza married Yale divinity professor Benjamin W. Bacon, DD, son of Reverend Leonard Woolsey Bacon, and had two children. Son

William, although paralyzed at age two, graduated from Norwich Free Academy and Amherst College and then returned to Norwich to read law. He was admitted to the bar in 1888 and practiced law until 1893, when his brother, John, died, leaving William to join the family firm, where he served as secretary until his death in 1903. Eliza's brother Alfred graduated from Yale in 1891 and became a banker in Massachusetts. He was president of the Worcester County Institution for Savings and president of the Massachusetts Bankers Association. He married Elizabeth Peck Hopkins of Worcester and had a son.

Second son John was educated at Norwich Free Academy and Massachusetts Institute of Technology. He worked at the Norwich Nickel & Brass Company from 1892 until his death in February 1893. Eliza's sister Edith Matson married Charles H. Palmer of Milwaukee, Wisconsin, in June 1897 and died in 1899, a year after the birth of a daughter. Eliza's sisters Jane and Mary lived at 157 Washington Street until about 1942 and then were listed at 188 Washington Street until Jane's death in 1949. In 1952, Mary moved to 33 Sachem Street and remained there until her death in 1959.

James Stedman Carew (1821–1881)

61/145 Washington Street

For more than fifty years, the Carew family lived in a stately home at the corner of Washington and Broad Streets. James S. Carew, a merchant and manufacturer, was mayor of Norwich when the Civil War began.

He was born on January 23, 1821, the son of Ebenezer (the second) and Sally (Eels) Carew, daughter of Edward and Mercy (Denison) Eels of Stonington. His older sister Lydia married I.M. Buckingham. In the 1850 census, Carew was enumerated with the Buckinghams. Later that year, he married Leonie Grandjean.

By the 1860 census, the Carews were living at 61 Washington Street, just north of the Buckinghams. By 1870, Carew had become president of Hayward Rubber Company (described in the census as a "rubber boot and shoe manufacturer"). His holdings totaled $400,000 ($103 million©). Son Charles was a clerk at the factory, young Leonia was at school and a second son, James, had joined the family. The household staff had grown to three domestic servants and a coachman.

Maps and newspaper articles indicate Carew owned considerable land over the years. At some point, he owned a parcel farther north on Washington Street, one or more wharves in the harbor and land adjacent to the wharves that was involved (with others) in a dispute and settlement with the railroad.

Carew was active in political and town affairs, and in 1860, he was elected mayor of Norwich. Mayor Carew presided over sometimes spirited city meetings in the early days of the Civil War. He was elected for a second one-year term but was defeated by his next-door neighbor J. Lloyd Greene, a "Union man," in 1862.

After her husband's death on July 16, 1881, Leonie remained at 145 Washington Street for about year and then moved to Norwich Town until her death in 1895.

Young James had been working at the Jewett City Mills, but apparently he moved to Michigan in the late 1880s. He appears in city directory listings in Detroit and, in the 1930 census, with his sister, Leonia Mclemman.

Charles joined his father and uncle in making rubber shoes and boots and, by 1880, had become secretary of Hayward Rubber Company. He married Jennie Allen in 1876, and around 1883, they moved to 145 Washington Street. Charles and his family occupied the house well into the twentieth century.

5

SENATOR LAFAYETTE S. FOSTER

H e was unanimously elected president pro temporare of the U.S. Senate, which set him up to become vice president of the United States.

LAFAYETTE SABINE FOSTER (1806–1880)

85/315 Broadway

Although he was never elected vice president of the United States, Lafayette Foster twice came within a heartbeat of the presidency. Had all the conspirators completed their assignments on April 14, 1865, Vice President Andrew Johnson would have been assassinated along with President Abraham Lincoln. Lafayette Foster, as president pro tempore of the Senate, would have become president of the United States.

A few months after he became president, Andrew Johnson contracted pneumonia and was near death. Foster, who was touring western Indian reservations with a congressional committee, was summoned back to Washington in anticipation of Johnson's death. But Lafayette Foster never became president.

Foster was born on November 22, 1806, in Franklin, Connecticut, the son of Daniel Foster and his second wife, Welthea (Ladd) Foster. His father was a direct descendant of Miles Standish, and his mother's family reached back

Above: Lafayette Foster's Italianate residence at 315 Broadway is now part of the Norwich Free Academy campus. *Courtesy of the author.*

Left: Lafayette S. Foster, acting vice president of the United States from 1865 to 1867. *Courtesy of Slater Memorial Museum.*

to colonial Connecticut. Captain Foster was a veteran of the Revolutionary War who served at Saratoga.

His father's death in 1822 prompted Foster to take responsibility for the care of his mother until her death in 1851.

Foster was educated at the local common schools and then studied in Hartford and Windham and taught two terms of school before entering Brown College (now University) in Providence in 1825. He graduated first (with top grades) in the class of 1828. For three years, Foster alternated teaching and studying law, notably with Norwich lawyer Calvin Goddard, the former congressman and state Supreme Court justice considered one of the best legal minds in the state.

Foster came to Norwich for good in 1832 and opened his law practice. His strong interest in politics led him to edit a newspaper, but when his growing practice didn't leave room for the attention a newspaper deserved, he gave it up.

On October 2, 1837, he married Joanna Boylston Lanman, daughter of James and Marion (Chandler) Lanman. Her father, a lawyer, served in the U.S. Senate from 1825 to 1831 and was a state Supreme Court justice. With the marriage, Foster became the uncle of Marianna Hubbard (later Mrs. John F. Slater), whose mother was Joanna's sister. The Fosters had three children, all of whom died in infancy. Foster felt the loss keenly and confided to a friend that he didn't want to leave Norwich because it would mean leaving the children.

More tragedy struck in 1859, when Senator Foster and his wife, Joanna, were shopping in Boston on Friday, April 8, and Mrs. Foster suffered what was called a "fainting fit." She asked to be taken home and, upon her return to Norwich, went to bed. Her illness didn't arouse concern until Sunday afternoon, and she died early Monday morning. A diary kept by niece Juliana Hyde, the daughter of Foster's sister, Welthea, and her husband, Augustus Hyde, described the incident, the family's shock and her uncle's sorrow during the difficult days following Joanna's death.

In October 1860, Senator Foster married Martha Prince Lyman, of Northampton, Massachusetts.

Foster was elected to the Connecticut General Assembly five times between 1839 and 1854. Members chose him Speaker of the House three times in that period and again in 1870, when he returned to the statehouse after leaving the U.S. Senate.

Although he was unsuccessful in two attempts to be elected governor, Foster was elected mayor of Norwich in 1851 and reelected by a unanimous vote in 1852. His disappointment about the gubernatorial election may have been mitigated by the award of an honorary doctor of law degree from Brown in 1851. Foster was elected again to the general assembly in 1854, and that body elected him U.S. senator from Connecticut on May 9. In the Senate, he chaired the committee on pensions and was a member of the committees on the judiciary, foreign relations and Indian affairs.

He was elected president pro tempore of the Senate in March 1865. Lafayette Foster became acting vice president of the United States a month later, when President Lincoln was assassinated on April 15. At the time, the president pro tempore followed the vice president in the line of presidential succession. Had George Adzerot completed his assignment and assassinated Vice President Johnson, Foster would have become president. Perhaps because of his position, Foster was one of the Senate pallbearers for Lincoln's funeral. They served as an honor guard; the casket was actually carried by military veterans.

By the 1860 census, although he had been in the Senate six years, Foster's occupation was still listed as lawyer. In 1870, he reported holdings of $113,000 ($29.1 million©), and his occupation was "Judge, Supreme Court." Enumerated with him and Martha were two servants and a gardener.

His contemporaries described Lafayette Foster as a gifted speaker and a charming, witty companion, courteous and gentlemanly but brimming with good humor.

Foster's career in the U.S. Senate coincided with the nation's greatest debate and the Civil War, and he was considered one of the first to recognize that war was, perhaps, inevitable. As early as 1854, in his first speech as Speaker of the Connecticut House, he framed the debate as being about "liberty and right, not slavery and might." In the Senate, Foster opposed every attempt to expand slavery beyond the limits of the Missouri Compromise.

Senator Foster advocated compensated emancipation of slaves in Missouri and the repeal of the Fugitive Slave Act in 1864, but in justice to slaveholding states that remained in the Union, he favored preserving the 1793 Fugitive Slave Act. He opposed giving the vote to African American residents of the District of Columbia because there was no educational qualification included in the bill.

In 1865, Foster was appointed a member of the Doolittle Congressional Committee to investigate the condition of the Indian tribes and their treatment by civil and military authorities of the United States. The committee members toured Kansas, Colorado and New Mexico, and as acting vice president, Foster was given a welcome as the greatest "Father" the tribesmen had ever seen. Years later, Senator Doolittle described the scene, in a letter to Martha Foster, as each of the chiefs greeted Foster with an enthusiastic embrace, followed by the women of the tribe. Since they were not as tall as the men, their painted faces rubbed against Foster's shirtfront, leaving the appearance that he wore "a coat of many colors," Doolittle wrote.

In Taos, New Mexico, they met with the famed frontiersman Kit Carson to obtain his viewpoint of the Indian situation. He and Senator Foster became close enough that after Carson's death, Foster offered to educate one of his sons.

It was during this trip that Andrew Johnson became so ill it was feared he would die. As the party returned to Denver, a messenger delivered urgent telegrams from Secretaries Seward and Stanton seeking Foster's immediate return to Washington. When he reached Denver, more telegrams awaited, saying Johnson's health was improved. Nevertheless, Foster was cautioned to remain in range of the telegraph.

It was expected that Foster would serve a third term in the Senate; however, the powers of the Republican Party in Connecticut objected that he was too close to President Johnson and also cited the traditional two-term limit, so he was not nominated.

Foster was philosophical about the loss of the third term in the Senate. "The loss of my election did not seriously affect my digestion, or my sleep, and will not, I fancy, affect the crops," he wrote in a letter to a friend. Later, he said the honors of his profession meant more to him than political honors.

He taught law at Yale, and in 1870, he was again elected to the state House of Representatives and chosen as Speaker of the House. But he resigned before the close of the session, when appointed to the Connecticut Supreme Court by a unanimous vote in the Connecticut Senate. Judge Foster served on the court until he reached the mandatory retirement age of seventy.

He was the first president of the New London County Historical Society and a longtime trustee at Norwich Free Academy. Although he was largely a protectionist, he was named an honorary member of London's free-trade Cobden Club and also was vice-president of the American Bible Society and a delegate of the Evangelical Alliance of the United States to Basil, Switzerland.

In 1880, Senator Foster was struck by the malarial fever that had bothered him for years. It wasn't serious for several days, but as the condition worsened, he became delirious and unconscious and died on September 19, 1880.

Foster's will contained bequests for Norwich Free Academy and the Yale Law School, to establish an endowed chair in common law. Another bequest provided an endowment for a prize for the best Greek scholar at Brown, which is still awarded today. In 1885, Mrs. Foster presented a marble bust of her husband to the U.S. Senate, which is now displayed in the vice president's room. She also commissioned a memorial biography of her husband, who always said he was too busy to write the story of his life.

Although she spent winters in the South, Martha Foster kept the house on Broadway as her primary residence until her death in 1903.

6

The Greenes and Benjamin W. Tompkins

The Greenes were among the earliest of Norwich's modern industrialists. Their mills became the nucleus of the city's first mill village, which was named Greeneville.

William P. Greene (1795–1864)

55/135 Washington Street

His father was one of the wealthiest men in Boston and president of the United States Bank, with antecedents going back to English statesman William Pitt. The family home on Pemberton Hill in Boston was renowned for its grounds and gardens. His stepmother was the daughter of artist John Singleton Copley.

William Parkinson Greene became wealthy in his own right by creating a manufacturing empire in Connecticut. He came to Norwich in 1824 to oversee his father's interests in the Thames Manufacturing Company along the Yantic River at the Norwich Falls. Greene was born in 1795 in Boston, the son of Gardiner and Elizabeth (Hubbard) Greene. He graduated from Harvard College in 1810 and then studied law, but poor health as a result of lung hemorrhages was thought to make that career too taxing for him.

William Greene married Augusta Elizabeth Borland, daughter of Leonard and Sarah Vassall Borland, on July 14, 1819. They became the parents of eight children.

William P. Greene was a founding director and first president of the Thames Bank and remained in that position for sixteen years. He was the first and largest contributor to a fund for improving water power along the Shetucket River and establishment of the Norwich Water Power Company. He also was among Norwich citizens who saw the advantage of a railroad line between Norwich and Worcester. Through his personal influence, the railroad obtained the credit of the Commonwealth of Massachusetts to build the track.

The Thames Company bought the Quinebaug Company cotton and woolen mill on the Shetucket River. With the purchase of a mill in Bozrah, the Thames Company was operating three large mills. The company failed in the panic of 1837, and Greene lost most of his personal fortune as well. A loan from his brother Benjamin allowed him to organize the Shetucket Company in 1838 with his brother and Samuel Mowry, a Greeneville machinist. They established the Norwich Falls Company in 1843 and then bought the Thames Company mill. With each mill running about 1,500 spindles, the venture proved profitable enough for William Greene to rebuild his fortune and repay his brother in a very short time.

Because of his health, Greene declined most appointments and attempts to involve him directly in Norwich's civic affairs, although he served a single term as mayor in 1841. His greatest civic commitment was as an original incorporator of Norwich Free Academy and his term as second president of its board of trustees, which he held until his death.

To commemorate the city bicentennial and Greene's birthday, which fell on the same day in 1859, his wife presented to the NFA a house on Broadway for use as the headmaster's residence. By 1864, the Greenes' other contributions to the academy reportedly totaled $40,000 (about $14,000,000©).

Augusta Greene died in 1861 and William in 1864 at the age of sixty-eight. It was said his advanced age was a testimony to his strength of will in the face of a lifetime of precarious health.

Elizabeth Greene, who never married, lived in her father's home and then with her brother Gardiner, where she was enumerated in the 1870 census with assets totaling $230,000 ($51.5 million©). She died in 1872 in Bordeaux, France. Daughter Augusta married General William G. Ely in 1865 and lived nearby in Norwich with their two children. In 1851, Anna Greene married John Jeffries, one of the first real estate brokers in Boston, where they raised their three children.

GARDINER GREENE (1822–1895)

139 Washington Street

Like his father, Gardiner Greene trained as a lawyer but spent most of his life as a manufacturer.

He was born in 1822 in Boston, Massachusetts, and came to Norwich as a child. After graduating from Yale College, he attended Harvard Law School and, degree in hand, returned to Norwich in 1845. His health was said to be too poor for him to follow the law, so Gardiner joined his father's company and was for many years the treasurer of both the Falls Company in Norwich and the Shetucket Company in Greeneville.

He was active in activities to improve the city and donated generously to fundraisers. He was a director of the Norwich Water Power Company and a trustee of the Thames Loan & Trust Company. The governor appointed him state commissioner of banking, but Greene's interests in Norwich banks precluded acceptance of the position. Though he didn't hold political office, he was counted as solidly Republican. A contemporary biography described Greene as "the soul of honor" with "a refined taste and pleasant unassuming manner."

In 1850, Greene married Mary Ricketts Adams of Alexandria, Virginia. Her father had been U.S. consul in Austria and Cuba, where he established a coffee plantation. Mary was described as devoted to her husband and family. They were the parents of two boys, Gardiner Jr. (1851) and Leonard V. (1858), who left Norwich for Cedar Rapids, Iowa, where he died in 1895.

The Greene family homes on Washington Street. Gardiner Greene's house (center) was razed, but J. Lloyd Greene's house at right still stands. James Carew, their neighbor, lived at the home on the far left. *Courtesy of Diane Norman.*

By 1870, Greene's fortune had increased to $200,000 ($51.5 million[©]). By then, his father had died, and he and his brothers were running the mills. In the census, his household included his wife, Mary; son Leonard; a coachman; three female servants; and his sister Elizabeth Greene.

The Greenes were members of Christ Episcopal Church, where Gardiner Greene was a vestryman and senior warden of the church.

In the late 1870s, the Greenes sold their home to David A. Wells. They moved to Norwich Town, and it was there that Gardiner Greene died in 1895 and Mary Adams Greene in 1906.

GARDINER GREENE JR. (1851–1925)

For a time, Gardiner Greene Jr. was the leader of Connecticut's Republican Party, and his legal training made him an obvious choice for a committee to overhaul state laws.

Greene graduated from Norwich Free Academy, then Yale University and finally Columbia College Law School. After some time in Utica, New York, he returned to Norwich as a partner of John T. Wait, a member of Congress from 1876 to 1887. After Wait's death in 1900, Greene continued the practice until he was appointed a judge of the Superior Court in 1909.

He twice served in the Connecticut House of Representatives and was chosen as leader of the Republican members. He was chosen to be House chairman but refused the seat. Greene was one of six attorneys chosen to revise the Connecticut State Statutes, and their revisions were adopted during the 1902 session.

He was a vice-president of the Dime Savings Bank, a trustee of the Berkeley Divinity School in Middletown and an incorporator of Norwich Free Academy. Like his father, Gardiner Jr. was a member of Christ Episcopal Church, where he was a junior warden.

He married Louise Eustis Reynolds in 1894. Her father, Henry Reynolds, was a Norwich native who moved to the South as a cotton broker just before the outbreak of the Civil War.

Gardiner Greene died in 1925 and Louise ten years later. They had no children.

JAMES LLOYD GREENE (1827–1883)

57/127 Washington Street

On at least two occasions, Norwich mayor James Lloyd Greene called for a cannon salute to mark an occasion. Both proved controversial.

The first, in 1863, was to mark the signing of the Emancipation Proclamation by President Abraham Lincoln. Then mayor Greene ordered all the city's bells to be rung for an hour in addition to a one-hundred-gun salute, which was believed to be the first public celebration of the proclamation in the state of Connecticut.

Not everyone supported the action, however. Five citizens obtained a court order to prevent the town from paying for the gunpowder, so Greene used his own money to pay the bill. A newspaper article of the time sneered, "He is a political relation of Lloyd Garrison's, probably."

The second salute cost Greene the governor's chair: a one-hundred-gun salute in 1874 to mark the successful suppression of White League combatants at Liberty Place in New Orleans became a symbol for his opponents in his 1875 campaign.

James Lloyd Greene was born in Norwich in 1827. Like his older brother, Gardiner, James joined his father's business and became an officer of the Falls and Shetucket Companies. By 1862, however, he had amassed a considerable fortune of $200,000 ($74.3 million©), and politics had become his major interest. In the census, he is variously identified as manufacturer, mayor or "no occupation."

J. Lloyd Greene, as he was known, was elected mayor for the first time in 1862. In a departure from tradition, the townspeople continued to reelect him until the end of the Civil War.

Like his father, Lloyd Greene was an original incorporator of Norwich Free Academy and also served as a trustee. He was a director of the Thames Fire Insurance Co. and Norwich Savings Society.

Greene married Matilda Smith in 1849 in Essex, Massachusetts, and they became the parents of six children. In the 1850 census, they were living with Greene's parents, perhaps to better supervise construction of their home at 57 (now 127) Washington Street. The house, it was said, was built under Greene's direct supervision at a cost of $80,000.

After Lloyd Greene's death in 1883, Matilda moved to Boston to live with daughter Margaret, who had married Charles Emerson Cook, a Harvard graduate and playwright. Her other daughters, Mary and Matilda, apparently never married and also lived with their sister during the early 1900s.

WILLIAM PARKINSON GREENE JR. (1831–1892)

64/170 Washington Street

As a young man, Will Greene became a neighborhood celebrity of sorts as the victim of an accidental shooting, and news of the incident went all the way to France. As an adult, he carried on his family's manufacturing legacy.

Will, the youngest of the Greene brothers, was born in Norwich in 1831. He was educated at Norwich Free Academy and Cheshire Academy, but poor health kept him from vigorous study, so he joined his father and brothers in the family manufacturing businesses.

The shooting incident occurred one summer day in 1852, and the incident was described by Emily Tyler in a letter to her daughter Gertrude, who was attending finishing school in Paris. Mrs. Tyler said Will was out shooting with a friend, whose pistol accidentally discharged and the ball grazed Greene's side.

"There was a terrible bustle about it, they had two Doctors and the whole neighborhood was quite alarmed, not much harm was done, but Will stalks

When he married Theodosia Tompkins, William P. Greene Jr. bought this house at 170 Washington Street, next door to her parents. *Photo by the author.*

around quite a Hero," Mrs. Tyler wrote. The account was published in a book about the Tyler family written by her granddaughter, Edith Carow (Mrs. T.R.) Roosevelt.

Two years later, Greene married Theodosia D. Tompkins, daughter of Benjamin and Eliza (Borman) Tompkins. It appears they lived for a time with her parents. Then in 1865, Greene paid $25,000 for the house next door, and that was the family's home for the next thirty years. By 1870, Greene had accumulated holdings of $165,000, and he and his family were living with two servants.

In 1879, when a group bought the Bozrah mills (apparently those owned by Greene's father-in-law) and established a new company, Will Greene became senior director of that firm while retaining his connection with the Greene family companies.

A contemporary biography indicates that Greene was a Republican and interested in civic affairs, but he declined nomination for political office. They were active in Center Congregational Church.

Theodosia died in 1896. Her husband survived her until June 7, 1898, when he died a week after son Benjamin's death on May 29. Daughter Augusta continued to live at 170 Washington Street until about 1911, when she moved to New York City.

BENJAMIN WILDMAN TOMPKINS (1808–1892)

66/172 Washington Street

Although not as well known today as some of the other residents of Norwich's Millionaires' Triangle, the name of Benjamin W. Tompkins was recognized in the nineteenth century. He was president of the Connecticut Temperance Society for years and an advocate of treatment for the mentally ill.

Tompkins was born in Southbury, Connecticut, in 1808, the son of Elihu Tompkins and Aletta (Osbourne) Tompkins. He was the owner of the Bozrahville Manufacturing Company in Bozrah, the town immediately adjacent to Norwich. He was connected with that firm from 1837 until his retirement about 1878.

While still in Southbury, he married Eliza Ann Borman. At some point, they moved to Middletown, where their daughter Theodosia was born in 1833.

The house at 172 Washington Street was the residence of mill owner Benjamin W. Tompkins, who was president of the Connecticut Temperance Society for many years. *Photo by the author.*

In 1866, Tompkins was appointed to a committee charged with overseeing construction of the state's first hospital for the insane. Until then, indigent mentally ill people were consigned to the almshouses, but it was nearly impossible to secure proper care for them, noted the announcement of the appointments. The first hospital was in Middletown, but it's likely that Tompkins's efforts led to construction of a facility in Norwich a few years later.

An 1871, a *Norwich Aurora* article took note of the remodeling at the Tompkins home, including replacement of the roof with a "French roof," presumably the mansard style on the house at present. The job included addition of a piazza in front and interior renovations.

Tompkins, a longtime deacon in the Congregational church, often preached at the chapel in Bozrahville. He was president of the National Congregational Council in Chicago in 1869. He also had been active in the American Social Science Association and temperance movements, serving as president of the Connecticut Temperance Society for many years.

Like many of the city's leaders, Tompkins took his turn serving in the state legislature and serving as a trustee of the Norwich Savings Society and director of the New London County Insurance Company. He was known for his generosity toward the poor.

When Governor and Senator William A. Buckingham died in 1875, Tompkins was a bearer at the funeral, identified in newspaper coverage as a "large manufacturer and intimate personal friend" of Senator Buckingham.

Tompkins died in 1892, after two years as an invalid. Eliza Tompkins died in 1900 at the age of ninety-two.

7

The Ballous, the Youngs and the Almys

Leonard Ballou's mills were actually in the village of Ballouville in Killingly, but he preferred to live in Norwich. That move gave the city a connection with an iconic jeweler.

Leonard Ballou (1794–1880)

73/171 Washington Street

Leonard Ballou was born on February 23, 1794, the eldest son of Noah and Abigail (Thurston) Ballou of Cumberland, Rhode Island. His ancestors were Huguenots from France who came to America for religious freedom and ultimately settled in the Roger Williams Colony, now Rhode Island. The family tree includes President James A. Garfield, who married Elizabeth Ballou.

Leonard Ballou was educated at the town school and was preparing for college when shipping embargoes damaged his father's business. Although he could have been a teacher, Leonard preferred to work with his hands and became a millwright who found himself in demand among the leading manufacturers of the day.

In 1822, Ballou married Ann Eliza Amsbury, daughter of Jabez Amsbury of Cumberland, and had two daughters (Lydia, 1823–1894, and Amelia, 1828–1887). Two years after Ann's death in 1852, Ballou married Dolly A.E. Kingsley. She died in 1862.

Textile manufacturer Leonard Ballou lived with his daughter Lydia and her husband, John Young, in this house at 171 Washington Street. Young was a cofounder of the New York jewelers Tiffany & Co. *Photo by the author.*

In 1825, the Ballous moved to Killingly, Connecticut, where Leonard and some Kingsbury family members transformed a gristmill into a small cotton mill, which they expanded into a major manufacturing operation.

Ballou began buying his own cotton in the early 1830s, and his foresight and careful management of the mills allowed them to weather economic downturns without losses. Ballou had doubled the mill capacity, and in 1836, he bought out his partners. The Ballou mills ran as many as twenty-six thousand spindles. Their location in Killingly became known as Ballouville.

It was a point of pride that Ballou never failed to repay his debts, always met payments when due and neither sued nor was sued by anyone. His mechanical background allowed him to evaluate new technologies to determine whether they would enhance his operations. His reputation for honesty and fair dealing extended to his employees as well as those with whom he did business.

Construction of the Norwich & Worcester Railroad in the 1840s opened opportunity for both acquisition of raw cotton and shipment of finished goods. Norwich also became a major transportation center and a very wealthy city populated by mill owners and other wealthy families.

In 1845, the Ballous moved to 171 and 183 Washington Street in Norwich. Daughter Amelia and her husband occupied one house and

Leonard the other. Although her husband's business was in New York, daughter Lydia Ballou Young spent much of her time with her father and sister, apparently preferring Norwich to New York.

Ballou retired in 1864 and sold his mills to his Washington Street neighbors Lorenzo Blackstone and the Norton brothers, who consolidated them into their Attawaugan Manufacturing Company.

Ballou was among the original incorporators of Norwich Free Academy in 1853. He was a director of the First National Bank and Norwich Fire Insurance Company and a trustee of the Norwich Savings Society and served on the Common Council in 1855. He was for four years president of the Norwich Water Power Company and, in his later years, served as a director of the Norwich Bleaching, Calendaring & Dyeing Company and president of the Occum Water Power Company. Ballou, a devout Congregationalist, was actively involved in establishment of Park Congregational Church and one of its largest contributors.

Leonard Ballou died in 1880 at the age of eighty-seven.

JOHN BURNETT YOUNG (1814–1859)

John Young and a friend had a dream. They would go to New York and open a store selling merchandise from China and Japan. With $1,000 borrowed from the friend's father, they carried out their plan. It was slow going at first, but they persisted and became not only successful but also the premier jewelers of New York, now known as Tiffany & Co.

John Burnett Young was born in Killingly, Connecticut, the son of Judge Ebenezer and Anna (Burnett) Young. His father was a lawyer, cloth manufacturer and probate judge who served in the Connecticut legislature and was a member of Congress from 1829 to 1835.

John B. Young went to Plainfield Academy, and it was there he and his friend Charles Lewis Tiffany decided to open a shop in New York. The twenty-five-year-olds borrowed $1,000 from Tiffany's father, another well-to-do mill owner in Killingly, and established a shop at 259 Broadway. At first their wares—items from China and Japan and costume jewelry—sold slowly.

Their merchandise was plainly marked, and they neither bargained nor haggled over the price, in contrast to other merchants of the day. They also had a "cash only" policy, unlike competitors who offered credit.

The new concept caught on, and by 1841, they took in another partner, J.L. Ellis, a Tiffany cousin, and became Tiffany, Young & Ellis. With the infusion of new money, Young went abroad on a buying trip and brought back a line of paste jewelry. It proved so popular that they decided to add more jewelry, including some real gold pieces. By 1845, the store carried only "the real thing," gold jewelry from London and Paris. Three years later, the partners started making their own gold items.

After the overthrow of the monarchy in 1848, the French economy collapsed. Young went to Paris with all the money he and his partners could gather and bought gems, including some of the crown jewels—pieces that had reputedly belonged to Marie Antoinette. Until then, diamonds had been rare in America, but Tiffany's promotion and marketing of the gems sent sales skyrocketing. Within ten years, Tiffany's was the largest diamond merchant in the country, and the press dubbed Tiffany "the King of Diamonds." Business flourished abroad as well, and the partners opened a branch store in Paris in 1850.

Meanwhile, both of the original partners married. Charles Tiffany married Harriet Olivia Avery Young, his partner's sister, in 1841. John Young married Lydia Ballou in 1842. A later partner, George McClure, the firm's gemologist, married another of John Young's sisters, Maria. When Tiffany's incorporated in 1868, McClure became secretary of the corporation.

When Tiffany bought out his partners and named the firm Tiffany & Co., John Young retired to Norwich, where his wife was looking after her widowed father. He settled into the community and joined his father-in-law as a director of the Norwich Fire Insurance Company.

John Young died in 1859. Although she and John never had children, Lydia Ballou Young wasn't alone in Norwich. Besides her father and her sister's family, there were other relatives nearby. Lydia almost certainly would have attended the marriage of her nephew Louis Comfort Tiffany to Mary Woodbridge Goddard of Norwich in 1872. Additionally, Lydia's nephew Leonard Ballou Almy married in 1876 and lived on Broad Street, a short distance away from his aunt, before moving into the Almy house next door. A year later, John Young's sister Ellen L. Peck, who had apparently separated from her husband, bought a house on Lincoln Avenue, about a quarter mile from the Ballous. There would have been other weddings, as the three Peck daughters married, and Lydia would likely have been at the marriage of Ellen B. Peck to William Slater in 1885.

Lydia Ballou Young survived her husband by more than thirty years. She died in 1894 at age seventy-one.

THE ALMY FAMILY

75/173 Washington Street

Members of the Almy family lived in this house for more than fifty years, often with multiple generations in residence at the same time.

Three generations of the Almy family lived in this house at 173 Washington Street. *Photo by the author.*

The patriarch was Albert Humphrey Almy, who was called Humphrey. During the Civil War, son John was assistant quartermaster general of the state, while son A.H. (Albert Henry) became an arms manufacturer. Another son, William (W.T.), was a merchant in Norwich.

Albert Henry (A.H.) Almy (1820–1906)

Albert Henry Almy, eldest son of Humphrey and Sarah Almy, was a newspaper financial editor who became a manufacturer.

He was born on August 3, 1820. Little is known about his early years and education. In 1847, Almy married Amelia Ballou, daughter of wealthy manufacturer Leonard Ballou, and moved into a house at 75 Washington Street, which was built by her father, who lived next door. Leonard Ballou Almy (1851) was the only one of their four children who survived to adulthood.

Almy was for years financial editor of the *New York Sun*. In Norwich, he was a director of the Norwich & Worcester Railroad, and in 1863, he was named president of the First National Bank, which was the second national bank chartered in Connecticut after Congress rewrote the banking laws. He was also an original incorporator of Norwich Free Academy.

During the Civil War, A.H. Almy was treasurer of the Eagle Manufacturing Company in Mansfield, Connecticut, and later an officer of the Norwich Arms Company. Through the influence of his brother John, who was assistant quartermaster general of the state, the company obtained a contract to produce rifles for the army. Almy teamed up with James Mowry, who also had an arms contract, to deliver the weapons.

The Almys variously lived at numbers 67, 73 and 75 Washington Street. It appears that family members moved among the houses as need or circumstances required. In any given census year, one or more Almys might be enumerated with Leonard Ballou.

The 1860 census enumerated Humphrey Almy, a merchant; his wife, Sarah; and son John, a twenty-nine-year-old merchant, still at home. A.H. Almy, an arms merchant; son Leonard; wife Amelia; and Amelia's newly widowed sister, Lydia B. Young, were living nearby at 73 Washington Street. By 1863, the city directory showed A.H. Almy living at 67 Washington, while his brother William was at 75 Washington and his father and Leonard Ballou were both at number 73. In 1870, A.H., Amelia Almy and Lydia Young were all enumerated with Leonard Ballou, perhaps because of earlier bankruptcy proceedings brought against Almy. The household also included Ellen A. Hutchins, age twenty-six, who is unidentified but may have been the visiting daughter of Dr. Samuel Hutchins of Killingly, a family connection. A coachman and two domestic servants complete the household listing. The A.H. Almys' eighteen-year-old son, Leonard, away at school, was enumerated in New Haven.

The family apparently had an active social life. There was a golden anniversary party to mark the fiftieth wedding anniversary of Humphrey and Sarah Almy, the first such celebration in the city. A scrapbook owned by Almy family descendants chronicles the family's activities from fishing and riding horseback, garden parties in the beautiful gardens behind the house to what the family called "Sunday parties"—apparently dinners—which continued until the house was sold after Dr. Leonard Almy's death.

There were visitors, too. Among them was Civil War general Ambrose Burnside, who stopped in on June 17, 1865, on the way to his home in Rhode Island. A newspaper report noted many citizens called on the general, who became governor of Rhode Island a year later.

Amelia Almy died unexpectedly in 1887, four days after her fifty-ninth birthday. Her death was a great loss, it was said, to not only her family but also the entire community. Albert H. Almy survived her until 1906.

Lieutenant Colonel Leonard Ballou Almy, MD. *Courtesy of Slater Memorial Museum.*

Leonard Ballou Almy (1851–1913)

Dr. Leonard Ballou Almy was Norwich's most notable soldier during the Spanish-American War.

He was born on July 17, 1851, the only survivor among his parents' four children. He attended private boarding schools and then Yale. After completing his medical training at Bellevue Medical College in New York, he spent a year studying in Europe before opening a practice.

In 1876, Dr. Almy married Caroline Stowell Webb, the daughter of Julius and Martha Webb, who lived on nearby Broad Street. Dr. and Mrs. Almy were the parents of two daughters.

Dr. Almy opened his practice in Norwich, where he became a successful and well-respected physician specializing in surgery. He was appointed chief medical examiner for New London County in 1883 and, a few years later, was named surgeon of Norwich's two railroads. Dr. Almy was instrumental in construction of the W.W. Backus Hospital and served as president, consulting surgeon and gynecologist for fifteen years before resigning in 1907, apparently for health reasons. Over the previous fifteen years, he had successively served as president of the city, county and state medical societies. Dr. Almy also was president of the Occum Water Power Company, which had been established to manage water rights along the Shetucket River.

Dr. Almy became surgeon of the Third Regiment, Connecticut National Guard, in 1886, and when the United States went to war with Spain, he became chief surgeon of the Connecticut State Volunteers with the rank of major; he became a lieutenant colonel and brigade medical director a few years later. During his army career, he wrote *Manual for Litter Drill for Hospital Corps*, intended for use with his brigade, which was later adopted for both state and national army use.

Shortly after the Spanish-American War began in 1898, he was commissioned as a major and served in several brigade assignments before being assigned to build and equip a seven-hundred-bed annex to the U.S. general hospital at Montauk Point, Long Island, New York. While there, he was injured and was honorably discharged from the army. For several years, Dr. Almy suffered from gangrene from the injury, which resulted in the amputation of his right leg in 1906 and the left six years later. Dr. Almy died in 1913, having survived his wife by about eighteen months.

Their daughter Lydia married Donald Chappell of New London in 1902. They divorced four years later, and she then married navy captain Wilson Brown, who became a decorated admiral; commander of the Naval Submarine Base in Groton, Connecticut; superintendent of the Naval Academy; and an advisor to three presidents. They had no children. Marguerite Almy married William Ellery Allyn of Groton in 1912. A World War I veteran, he was active in Connecticut State Republican politics and was president of the Norwich Water Power Company for a time. They moved to Waterford, where they lived at Oaklawn Farm for many years. Marguerite Almy Allyn was among the founders of the Waterford Public Health Nursing Service and the Waterford Library, and she was the last surviving founder of the New London Garden Club. The Allyns had two daughters.

8

GENERAL WILLIAM WILLIAMS AND MRS. HARRIET WILLIAMS

G eneral and Mrs. Williams were among the area's major philanthropists. Always concerned about education, the general donated the land for Norwich Free Academy, and Mrs. Williams provided funding for the library. She also donated land, a memorial window, bell chimes and the clock tower for the new Park Congregational Church. With no heirs at her death, she financed funding of a private school, now the Williams School in New London, where the family had business interests for many years.

GENERAL WILLIAM WILLIAMS (1788–1870) AND HARRIET PECK WILLIAMS (1795–1880)

Williams Park/9 Chelsea Parade South

For more than a quarter of its two hundred years, the stately three-story Federal-style brick mansion at the foot of Chelsea Parade was the home of General William Williams and his wife, Harriet Peck Williams.

The house overlooks the parade grounds where General Williams and others drilled their militia troops. For years, the tree-bordered triangular parcel was known as Williams Park for its proximity to the Williamses' residence. It was surrounded by the homes of some of the city's most prominent residents.

The residence of General Williams and Harriet Williams overlooks Chelsea Parade. *Photo by the author.*

Left: Harriet Peck Williams was a philanthropist in her own right. *Courtesy of Slater Memorial Museum. Right*: General William Williams was a soldier, a merchant and a philanthropist. *Courtesy of Slater Memorial Museum.*

The house was built in 1789 for Joseph Teel, who operated it as a tavern called the Teel House, Sign of General Washington. The house boasts a third-floor assembly room that saw a range of activities, including club and lodge meetings, shows and balls. The floor is gimbaled, or set on springs to absorb the shock of dancing feet.

William Williams was born in 1788 in Stonington, Connecticut, the son of William and Mercy (Wheeler) Williams. His mother died when he was young, so he and his brother, Thomas, were sent to Plainfield Academy. In 1802, the fourteen-year-old William went to New York City and worked in a commission house to learn the shipping merchant's trade, and at eighteen, he went to sea on one of his father's ships. For two years, he was the supercargo, overseeing business matters and the sale and purchase of the merchandise for the vessel.

After moving to Norwich in 1809, Williams ran a corn- and wheat-grinding mill and then manufactured cotton. At heart, though, he was a shipping merchant, and over the next six years, his ships had many successful voyages to Europe and South America. In 1828, Williams and Captain Acors Barns of New London began a whaling and commission business, which lasted until Williams's death in 1870. Williams & Barns was said to be a major factor in New London's reputation as a whaling port.

As a young man, William Williams was active in the state militia, attaining the rank of major general, and he was almost universally addressed as "General" throughout his life.

In 1812, General Williams married Harriet Peck, the daughter of Captain Bela Peck, a wealthy Norwich Town businessman. She and her sister, Charlotte, were educated at the Moravian Seminary School in Bethlehem, Pennsylvania. Of the Williamses' three sons, only Thomas reached adulthood and became a partner in Williams & Barns. Thomas Wheeler Williams II died quite suddenly in 1855 at age forty, leaving his wife, Amanda, widowed without a family, as all four of their children died as infants. Amanda died a few years later.

When the Merchants Bank was organized in 1833, General Williams was among the original incorporators and was the bank's first president until he resigned twenty-five years later. He was a board member of the American Board of Commissioners for Foreign Missions and also vice-president of the Bible, Seamen's Friend and Home Missionary societies.

General Williams was a deeply religious man and prominent member of the Congregational Church. He was also interested in the moral and religious well-being of the Mohegan Indians and made weekly trips to teach Sunday school at their reservation a few miles from Norwich.

Among other holdings, General Williams owned much of the land along what is now Williams Street and parcels along Broadway. In the 1850 census, he reported owning real estate worth $30,000, or $14 million© in 2012. A board of trade list of the city's wealthiest men in 1865 put his annual income at $23,293 ($4.25 million© in 2012). By 1870, General Williams still held $50,000 in real estate and $50,000 of personal estate. Mrs. Williams separately reported $50,000 in real estate and $50,000 of personal estate, putting their joint holdings at about $52 million today. Their household in 1870 included two domestic servants and a coachman.

By all accounts, the general and his lady were a loving and devoted couple. They marked their fiftieth wedding anniversary in 1862 with a gala celebration, which was deemed important enough to be chronicled in Caulkins's *History of Norwich*, published only a few years later.

General and Mrs. Williams were well known for their interest in educational matters. In addition to donating seven acres of land for the school, he was an original incorporator of Norwich Free Academy and served as the third president of NFA's board of trustees. Mrs. Williams contributed $5,000 for a library to be named the Bela Peck Library, in honor of her father, with additional funding for books. She also established several prizes for scholarship.

General Williams died on October 28, 1870, leaving his widow the last of her family. Mrs. Williams continued her many acts of private charity, including donation of land for Park Congregational Church.

When Mrs. Williams died on October 14, 1880, much of her fortune was left to establish a girls' high school in New London in honor of her son, Thomas. It is now the co-ed institution known as the Williams School on the campus of Connecticut College.

9

The Hubbards

The Hubbards were another of the early manufacturing families. Additionally, they published the city's newspaper, the *Norwich Courier*.

James Lanman Hubbard (1832–1890)

49 and 68/242 Broadway

James Lanman Hubbard was born in Norwich on December 25, 1832, the son of Amos Hallam and Eliza (Lanman) Hubbard.

In 1854, he married Charlotte Peck Learned, daughter of Ebenezer Learned and Harriet (Vail) Townsend Learned. Their children were Charles Learned (1855–1918) and Matilda D. (1858–1866). James's sister Marianna was married to wealthy manufacturer John F. Slater and lived on an estate across Broad Street from the Hubbard property. Their aunt Joanna Lanman, wife of Senator Lafayette Foster, lived just up the street near the Free Academy.

The Hubbard manufacturing interests began in 1818, when James's father, Amos Hallam Hubbard, established a paper mill on the Yantic River at the Norwich Falls. Within a few years, Amos replaced the manual process with machines, and by 1830, he had one of the first Fourdrinier papermaking machines in the state. Amos and his brother, Russell, publisher of the *Norwich*

This house at 242 Broadway was the home of paper manufacturer James L. Hubbard and later his son, Charles. *Photo by the author.*

Courier, formed a partnership for making paper, which lasted until Russell's sudden death in 1857. In 1860, Amos Hubbard sold the factory to William P. Greene and moved the papermaking operation to the village of Greeneville a few miles to the east.

After they married, James, Charlotte and young Charles lived on Main Street with his parents. By 1861, James Hubbard was living at 49 Broadway, on the corner of Otis Street. In 1869–70, he moved to 68 (later 242) Broadway after E. Winslow Williams moved to Yantic. By 1870, his mother was living just behind him, at 6 (now 24) Broad Street, and his sister was just across Broad Street at the Slater mansion. The 1873 tax list showed James Hubbard with an annual income of $39,500, or $9.74 million© in 2012.

In addition to his manufacturing interests, Hubbard was an original incorporator of the Thames Loan and Trust Company, established in 1869 to deal in stocks, bonds and securities for trusts and estates. He had already followed his father (a founder in 1825) as a director of the Thames National Bank in 1855.

James Hubbard died in December 1890, followed by Charlotte a few months later in August 1891.

CHARLES LEARNED HUBBARD (1855–1918)

68/242 Broadway

Charles Learned Hubbard was born in 1855. He was educated in local schools, graduated from Yale and immediately joined the family business. In 1877, he married Catherine A. Mather, the daughter of Captain Samuel W. and Frances Mather of Lyme, Connecticut. Captain Mather, a wealthy sea captain, had discovered the fastest route to Australia before he died in a Civil War firefight off the Florida coast in 1862. The Hubbards had four children, two of whom died young.

Like his cousin Will Slater and their neighbors the Osgood brothers, Charles Hubbard owned yachts and belonged to the New York Yacht Club. In 1893, he took delivery on a ninety-foot schooner-rigged steam yacht named *Kalolah* built at the Herreshoff Manufacturing Company in Bristol, Rhode Island. He was also an early automobile owner. Both Charles and his son, James, appeared on a 1903 list of motor vehicles registered in Connecticut.

By 1910, Charles Hubbard had almost certainly succeeded Slater as the wealthiest man in Norwich, and this was reflected in the census, which showed seven servants, including three cooks, two chauffeurs, a doorman and a general workman. Four of the servants were Japanese. The Hubbards' daughter, Rosalie, had married Huntington Lee in 1907, leaving her twenty-three-year-old brother, James, at 242 Broadway with his parents.

Hubbard's financial interests were not limited to paper manufacturing. He was president of Thames National Bank, and in 1908, he and his brother-in-law Huntington Lee bought a half-interest in W.W. Gale & Co., an electrical contracting company in New Haven. By 1912, they were sole owners of the firm, which installed electricity in major buildings in Norwich, New Haven and other Connecticut towns and also in Massachusetts.

Hubbard began manufacturing textiles and gained enough recognition in the industry that in October 1917, he traveled to Adams, Massachusetts, to act as an honorary bearer in the funeral of William B. Plunkett, a wealthy paper and textile manufacturer who was a personal friend of President William McKinley.

Hubbard was very active in the Masonic organization. He was a thirty-third-degree Mason and had been grand commander of the Knights Templar.

Charles L. Hubbard died of apoplexy in 1918 while visiting his son, James, a navy ensign, in Newport, Rhode Island. After his death, Catherine moved to New Haven, perhaps to be near Rosalie and her family. After his return from the service, James and his family settled on Scotland Road.

10

THE ELYS

J esse Ely probably knew better than anyone just how wealthy people in Norwich were, since he had the responsibility of collecting tax revenues in Connecticut's Third District. His son William became a soldier and was a man of great perseverance—he and his men escaped from a Confederate prison camp by digging a tunnel.

JESSE SANFORD ELY

63/231 Broadway

Jesse Sanford Ely was a merchant, revenue collector and manufacturer who came to Norwich from Killingly, Connecticut. He was born in 1807, the son of Eli and Sarah Ely, and in 1835, he married Harriet Grosvenor, daughter of Dr. Robert and Mary Grosvenor and had three children.

They came to Norwich around 1850 and opened a dry goods store. He was an original incorporator and director of the Uncas Bank in 1852, joining such prominent men as William P. Greene, Henry B. Norton and William Buckingham. Ely was president of the bank for at least five years before he died in 1879.

By the 1860 census, the Ely household included Harriet; William, twenty-five, a civil engineer; Edwin, nineteen, a clerk; and two servants.

Jesse Ely, merchant and federal revenue assessor, lived at 231 Broadway. *Photo by the author.*

In 1862, Jesse Ely was appointed the first federal revenue assessor for the Third Congressional District. After four years, someone else was appointed to the political position, but Ely was reinstated a short time later. In his later life, Jesse Ely was a paper manufacturer and ran mills in Baltic and Versailles until his death in 1879.

The Elys' son Edwin married Mary Brewer Chappell in 1873, and they had four children. She was the daughter of Elizabeth (Brewer) and Edward Chappell, the wealthy owner of Chappell Lumber and Coal in Norwich. Edwin became owner and manager of the Reade & Obenauer Paper Company in nearby Versailles. Health problems forced him to sell his interest in the mill in 1889. He was president of the Uncas Bank and a director of the Broadway Theater Corporation

WILLIAM GROSVENOR ELY

81/297 Broadway

William G. Ely was nothing if not determined. As an army captain, he spent twenty-seven hours straight in the saddle. As a colonel, he led a regiment that fought so bravely that the Confederate commander returned Ely's sword as a token of respect. And as a captive, he used whatever was available to tunnel out of the prison and escape.

Ely, the eldest son of Jesse and Harriet Ely, was born in 1836 in Killingly. He graduated from Brown University in Providence, Rhode Island, where he trained as a civil engineer. After graduation, he worked for the Rogers Locomotive Works in New Jersey and was sent to Cuba to represent their interests.

At the start of Civil War in April 1861, he returned to Norwich to enlist. Ely was commissioned a captain and was at First Manassas that summer with the First Regiment, Connecticut Volunteers. A news dispatch from the front noted that Captain Ely, who as an aide of Colonel Keys spent twenty-seven hours in the saddle, merited mention in official reports. Within six months, Ely was promoted to lieutenant colonel of the Sixth Regiment, Connecticut Volunteers.

When the Eighteenth Regiment was formed in 1862 with recruits from New London and Windham Counties, Ely was promoted to full colonel and given command of the regiment. During its first battle at Winchester, Virginia, in June 1863, the regiment was outnumbered by Confederates, and Colonel Ely was among those taken prisoner. In recognition of the brigade's bravery and courage during the fighting, Confederate general James Walker

General W.G. Ely commanded the Eighteenth Connecticut Regiment during the Civil War. *Courtesy of the author.*

returned Ely's sword, which had been struck and broken during the battle. Colonel Ely was among the men who used crude implements to dig a tunnel and escape from the prison, but he was recaptured about forty miles away. He was returned to prison until exchanged and paroled in March 1864.

When relieved of parole two months later, Colonel Ely rejoined the army and was given command of a brigade. At the Battle of Piedmont in June 1864, he was wounded in the throat and resigned from the army because of the disability. He was later brevetted a brigadier general.

In January 1865, General Ely married Augusta Greene, the daughter of Augusta and the late William P. Greene, and a member of the wealthy textile manufacturing family. They had two children.

While William Ely was fighting in the war, Augusta Greene had been making her own contributions to the cause. Besides her activities with the Ladies' Aid in securing supplies for the men at the front, she hired a substitute to serve as her representative in the army, the first woman to do so in Connecticut. She was honored with a certificate from the state legislature.

In 1868, General Ely was apparently sufficiently recovered from his war wound to join the Allen Manufacturing Company, a manufacturer of printing press machinery. By 1880, forty-eight-year-old William Ely had joined the Greene family firm and was treasurer of the Falls and Shetucket companies, and he held that position for many years.

The general died in 1908. Anna Ely never married, and after her parents' deaths, she lived for about twenty years in Norwich Town. Then, in about 1930, she moved to 11 Joseph Perkins Road, where she lived until her death. William Jr. graduated from Brown in 1892 with a PhD in electrical engineering and moved to Schenectady, New York, where he worked for General Electric Co. until he retired. He married and had three children.

Old maps indicate the Elys' house at 81 Broadway was just south of the home of A.W. Prentice (now the Allis House administration building on the NFA campus). The house was razed and the site incorporated into the campus.

11

THE LEE FAMILY

After escaping execution in England through the intervention of a future king, Benjamin Lee came to America, where he founded a family that included noted physicians, soldiers, statesmen and the first Episcopal bishop of the United States.

ELIZABETH GORHAM (LEIGHTON) LEE (1776–1871) AND BENJAMIN LEE (1765–1828)

52/118 Washington Street

For sixty years, Madame Elizabeth Lee was the grande dame of Washington Street. She and her husband bought 52 (later 118) Washington Street in 1811, and she remained in the house until her death in 1871.

In one anecdote, Madame Lee's granddaughter Edith Roosevelt described a Norwich woman who was vigorously cleaning her house. A friend asked, "Are you expecting a visit from Queen Victoria or Madame Lee?"

The story appeared in *American Backlogs*, Mrs. Roosevelt's family history of her mother, Gertrude Lee Tyler. In addition to genealogical information, the book included letters Mrs. Lee exchanged with her granddaughter while Gertrude was at school in France. She wrote loving

Madame Elizabeth Lee lived at 118 Washington Street for more than fifty years. *Photo by the author.*

letters filled with familial concern for a child an ocean away tempered with neighborhood gossip and the occasional acerbic comment (a visit from a Mrs. Cowen, who was "as fat as ever").

Benjamin Lee was born in England and served for a time in the Royal Navy, resigning after a fight with a shipmate that resulted in a death sentence. A royal prince, who was later King William IV, intervened, and the sentence was commuted. Lee moved to Cambridge, Massachusetts, where he joined his brother's firm, becoming a ship captain at nineteen.

He married Elizabeth Gorham Leighton in 1797 and lived in Cambridge, where their house was the subject of Henry Wadsworth Longfellow's poem "The Old House by the Lindens."

After his brother's death, Lee came to Norwich in 1812 and bought the elegant house as a summer residence, but he moved to live full time in Norwich after taxes tripled on his Cambridge property.

Benjamin Lee died in 1828 in Skaneateles, New York, where he owned considerable property and a place he used as a summer home.

The Lees were the parents of eight children, two of whom died in infancy. Their son Alfred became the first Episcopal bishop of Delaware and later presiding bishop of the Episcopal Church in the United States.

In Norwich, Elizabeth Lee was surrounded by her daughters. Two houses to the north lived Emily, who married Daniel P. Tyler, a soldier who became a railroad magnate. Mary wed wealthy attorney William Law. After Mary's death, William and his second wife lived just south of the Lee mansion for thirty years. Daughter Elizabeth moved to Springfield, Massachusetts, when she married James S. Dwight, the son of a wholesale merchant whose family used their own fleet of ships to stock their stores in Massachusetts and Connecticut. After his death in 1831, she returned to Norwich with her three young daughters, married John Turvil Adams and lived a short distance north of the mansion. Before she died in 1865, Elizabeth had knit one hundred pairs of socks for Union soldiers and was knitting yet another pair the night before her death.

Madame Lee died in 1871 at the age of ninety-four. The house was sold shortly after her death to A.P. Sturtevant and later used as a parsonage for Christ Episcopal Church.

12

ALBERT P. STURTEVANT

When Albert P. Sturtevant came to Norwich, he was a relatively young man planning to retire. About two years later, Sturtevant was back in business and making more money than ever in manufacturing, real estate and hotels.

ALBERT P. STURTEVANT

52/118 Washington Street

A.P. Sturtevant was born in 1817 in Centre Harbor, New Hampshire, the son of Perez and Dorothy (Kimball) Sturtevant. He became a carpenter, accumulated some capital and made a fortune as a builder and contractor. He married Eliza Dunbar in Norwich in 1838, and they had three children.

In June 1860, the census shows Alfred Sturtevant, a builder, living in New York City with Eliza, their son and two daughters. The family moved to Norwich during July 1860 and were enumerated a second time in August on the same page as Laurel Hill founder and resident Henry Bill.

About two years after arriving in Norwich, Sturtevant began acquiring mills in Norwich, East Lyme and Preston. He also was a director of the Middlesex Mutual Assurance Co. in Middletown.

In 1870, the census showed A.P. Sturtevant, manufacturer of woolens, and Eliza with their daughters and two servants in the household, which had moved to 50 Washington Street. They moved next door to the Lees' house in 1873–74.

Besides operating the mills, Sturtevant owned the Sturtevant House at Broadway and Twenty-ninth Street in New York, the Fort Griswold House and Edgecomb House in Groton and the Wauregan House in Norwich. News stories about the hotel invariably referred to A.P. Sturtevant as a "real estate millionaire."

In 1883, Sturtevant invented a fire escape that attracted considerable press coverage. Hotel employees demonstrated its use by exiting a sixth-story window. A long rope ran through a hook secured to the window, and a belt attached to the other end of the rope was fastened around the waist of the user and passed through a rubber tube, which the person grasped to control the rate of descent.

The Sturtevant household had grown considerably by the 1880 census: A.P. and Eliza with both daughters and their husbands. Florence had married William K. Shew and had a daughter. Shew was proprietor of the Wauregan House and later managed another Sturtevant hotel. After his wife's death, Shew moved to the Wauregan and placed his daughter as a ward in the home of druggist Nathan Sevin on Union Street.

Adeline had married Alfred S. Bolles, variously identified as a lawyer and editor of the *Norwich Bulletin*. After their marriage in 1874, he promptly took her on a cruise to Algeria. After Bolles's death, Adeline married James C. Matthews. Despite starting his hotel career only three years before, by 1886, Matthews was leasing the Sturtevant Hotel from his father-in-law and later managed the Fort Griswold Hotel.

Newspapers reported A.P. Sturtevant seriously injured in July 1892, when he was thrown from a carriage after it was struck by a streetcar. Although the injuries were initially considered fatal, he recovered, but died the following March.

It was believed his holdings, many of which were in New York real estate, totaled more than $2 million ($186 million[©]). It took more than fifteen years to settle the Sturtevant estate amid charges of malfeasance on the part of the executors, who countered that Sturtevant's business affairs were very tangled. The siege began with son Charles's attempt to declare his mother incompetent to manage such a large fortune; Adeline declared their mother perfectly competent. By 1902, creditors were in court seeking an accounting of the estate, which reportedly had liabilities of $500,000.

Additional complications came from claims against Adeline's husband, J.C. Matthews, who had borrowed from Sturtevant against the furnishing and fixtures of the Sturtevant House hotel. Matthews died in 1901, embroiled in lawsuits over his father-in-law's estate and repayment of debts related to the hotels.

By 1906, Adeline (Sturtevant) Matthews claimed to be reduced to living on her seven-dollar weekly salary at a cleaning and dyeing agency because she had never been able to get the executors to close out the estate.

Although the Sturtevant House Hotel sold in 1903 for $1.2 million, the estate executors placed the value of the estate at only $134,000 because of the liabilities against it.

Charles Sturtevant remained in East Lyme, where he became a respected businessman, was active in fraternal societies and served in the state Senate. He married Anna Elizabeth Smith in 1869, and they had four children. Charles died in 1898.

13

GENERAL DANIEL P. TYLER

After he left the army, Daniel Tyler applied his engineering background to railroads and manufacturing. When the Civil War broke out, he again became a soldier and later was again a manufacturer.

His large family included soldiers, manufacturers and a president's wife.

DANIEL PUTNAM TYLER (1799–1882)

56/130 Washington Street

Daniel P. Tyler was a talented artilleryman, an iron manufacturer and a railroad man. He was a general during the Civil War, and ten years after its end, he founded a town in the Deep South.

He was born on January 7, 1799, in Brooklyn, Connecticut. His father, Daniel P. Tyler III, was a Revolutionary War officer and son-in-law of General Israel Putnam, the hero of Bunker Hill. His mother, Sarah (Edwards) Chaplin, descended from Jonathan Edwards, the great theologian.

Tyler was educated at the Plainfield Academy and graduated from the U.S. Military Academy at West Point in 1819. Over the next fifteen years, Lieutenant Tyler distinguished himself as an expert on light artillery. His translations of French works on drill, maneuvers and field artillery and the information he gathered from them became the foundation for U.S. Army practices.

The house at 130 Washington Street belonged to General Daniel Tyler. His granddaughter Edith Carow Roosevelt, wife of President Theodore Roosevelt, was born here in 1861. *Photo by the author.*

In 1832, Tyler married Emily Lee, daughter of Benjamin and Elizabeth Lee of Norwich, and had five children.

By 1834, Tyler was an iron manufacturer in Pennsylvania, where he built the first coke hot-blast furnace in the United States and operated rolling mills. The business wasn't profitable, however, so the family returned to Norwich.

Tyler, a civil engineer, then became involved with railroads and transportation. During the 1840s, he saved the Norwich & Worcester Railroad from bankruptcy and revived railroads in New Jersey, Pennsylvania, Kentucky and Georgia.

His stature as a man of wealth is confirmed by his presence on the list of original incorporators of Norwich Free Academy.

When the Civil War began in 1861, Tyler was appointed lieutenant colonel of the First Connecticut Regiment. As the sole professional soldier, he was charged with preparing Connecticut's volunteer soldiers for wartime military service. Their discipline, training and equipment drew favorable notice from army commander-in-chief General Winfield Scott. Tyler was soon promoted to brigadier general and given command of a division in the Army of Northeastern Virginia. His actions during the First Battle of Bull Run sparked controversy over whether he followed the orders of his commanding officer. He was, in any case, promoted with postings in Mississippi, Virginia and Delaware.

On May 25, 1859, the Tylers' eldest son, Alfred, married Annie E. Scott, of Macon, Georgia, and they had three children. Alfred became president of the Anniston Manufacturing Company in the Alabama town his father helped found after the war. Three weeks after Alfred's wedding, his sister Gertrude married Charles Carow, the son of a New York shipping and mercantile family. Gertrude returned home in August 1861 for the birth of their daughter Edith (who would become the wife of U.S. president Theodore Roosevelt).

As an adult, Edmund Leighton Tyler, a graduate of West Point, lived in Anniston, Alabama and New London. He married Belle Alston Webb in Washington, D.C., on March 16, 1892, and had three children. Mary Law Tyler married Colonel Alexander Moore, an Irish native living in New York City, and had a son, who became one of President Roosevelt's military aides.

Augustus Cleveland Tyler followed his father and brother to West Point, where his father's efforts to secure his admission were the subject of an 1870 congressional investigation. Until 1878, Augustus served in the army at frontier posts in the West. He returned to Norwich in 1878 to marry Cornelia Osgood, daughter of the wealthy druggist Dr. Charles and Sarah (Larned) Osgood. After resigning the regular army, Augustus Tyler commanded the Third Regiment of the Connecticut National Guard. The Tylers and their three children lived in the South during the winter and summered in New London.

General Tyler resigned his commission in 1864, a month after his wife Emily died on March 9. Although he kept the Norwich house until 1868, he moved to Red Bank, New Jersey, which became his base during his extensive travels in the United States and abroad.

In 1872, while visiting his son Alfred in South Carolina, Tyler met Samuel Noble, whose description of iron ore deposits in Alabama piqued the Tylers' interest. Later, General Tyler and his two eldest sons joined Noble to establish the Woodstock Iron Company and the town of Anniston, Alabama (named for Tyler's younger son's wife, Annie). The general moved to Mobile, where he became president of the Mobile & Montgomery Railroad and offered counsel and backing for establishment of the town around the mill.

General Tyler continued to travel, frequently visiting Saratoga, New York, in the summer and spending his winters at his twenty-thousand-acre Texas ranch overseen by daughter Mary and her husband.

General Tyler died in 1882 while visiting New York City. As he wished, his body was taken to Anniston for burial.

A lengthy profile in the *Anniston Star* quoted General William Tecumseh Sherman, who served under Tyler at Bull Run. He said Tyler had "outspoken, enthusiastic devotion to his Country and Government in war and in peace…He was without one misstep or act of hesitation as a man, a soldier and gentleman."

DAVID A. WELLS

In 1870, the man who showed Abraham Lincoln how to finance the Civil War debt came to live in Norwich. From here, he traveled across the United States and to Europe to lend his financial acumen to governments and railroads with economic dilemmas.

DAVID AMES WELLS (1828–1898)

59/137 Washington Street

David Ames Wells had been a newspaperman, inventor, college professor and writer of science textbooks, but he was best known for his work in economics.

Wells was born on June 17, 1828, in Springfield, Massachusetts, the son of Rebecca (Ames) and James Wells, a manufacturer. His father's family was locally prominent, and his mother's Ames relatives became quite wealthy manufacturing shovels during the California gold rush and tools and swords during the Civil War. Her cousins Oakes and Oliver Ames were involved in building the Union Pacific Railroad and the related Crédit Mobilier scandal.

Wells graduated from Williams College in 1847 and published his first book, a history of the college. While working at a Springfield newspaper, he invented a machine to fold newspapers. He left Springfield for graduate

Internationally acclaimed economist David A. Wells moved to this house at 137 Washington Street about 1880. *Courtesy of the author.*

work at Harvard and then taught physics and chemistry and wrote science textbooks for G.P. Putnam & Son, the New York publisher.

His economics career was launched from Troy, New York, where he belonged to a literary society. At a meeting in 1863, Wells read his paper "Our Burden and Our Strength," in which he laid out a plan for retiring the huge debt amassed by the nation to finance the Civil War. Wells's paper was published as a pamphlet, with 200,000 copies circulated at home and abroad. In Norwich, I.M. Buckingham, the governor's brother, was so impressed that he had the pamphlet reprinted and circulated at his own expense.

President Abraham Lincoln learned of Wells's work and brought him to Washington to discuss the direction of nation's postwar economic policies. He appointed Wells chairman of a three-member revenue commission whose recommendations on taxation became law in 1866.

Wells advocated reducing taxes on liquor, which dramatically increased tax revenues. He advocated a federal Bureau of Statistics to gather economic and financial statistics that could be used to shape tax policy. Wells also played a role in the debate on tariffs, arguing that American manufacturing had become so strong that imported goods no longer posed a threat and tariffs were unnecessary—a complete reversal of his own original position.

When President U.S. Grant declined to renew Wells's appointment, congressmen from both political parties gave a testimonial for Wells, citing the value of his work and his integrity and zeal. New Jersey and New York underscored the point with a thirty-inch-high bronze statue of a workman titled *Labor*.

In 1870, Wells and his family settled in Norwich, where his wife had lived with her mother and stepfather. Her grandmother Elizabeth Lee still lived on Washington Street, a short distance across the river from Laurel Hill, the new community where they lived for several years. He had married Mary Sanford Dwight of Springfield on May 9, 1860, and their son, David, was born on April 27, 1868. The 1870 census showed the family in Norwich with a nurse and two domestic servants. Mary died shortly after they arrived in Norwich. Her sister, Ellen Dwight, became Wells's second wife on June 10, 1879. That marriage was without issue.

By 1880, the Wells family lived on fashionable Washington Street, in the house previously owned by Gardiner Greene Sr. The census showed a household consisting of Wells, Ellen, David, a gardener, a cook, a waitress and a laundress.

After he left government service, Wells was much sought after as a consultant for tax and railroad issues. The State of New York promptly hired him to investigate the loss of tax revenue to neighboring states and tolls on canals.

In 1876, a federal court appointed Wells a trustee and receiver for the Alabama & Chattanooga Railroad. It took just over a year for Wells to put the finances straight and make improvements without incurring debt. A few years later, he masterminded reorganization of the New York & Erie.

International accolades were showered on Wells. In 1874, he became a foreign associate of the French Academy, filling the vacancy created by the death of John Stuart Mill. He also garnered a degree from Oxford University and recognition from the Royal Statistical Society, London's Cobden Club and an Italian honors society. Wells was appointed to the board of visitors at West Point and became president of the American Social Science Association. He served as an economic adviser to Presidents James A. Garfield (a close friend) and Grover Cleveland. Wells himself unsuccessfully ran for Congress in 1876 and 1890.

Locally, Wells became the second president of the New London County Historical Society in 1880.

Wells was a prolific author; the Library of Congress has nine thousand items of his books, pamphlets and other writings, as well as correspondence with many of the important figures of his day.

Wells died at his home in 1898. He had been weakened by failing health and couldn't fight what appeared to be a cold. His son died of typhoid fever nineteen months later.

Wells was highly regarded among economists, and his works are still studied into the twenty-first century. At Harvard University and Williams College, there are endowed faculty positions in Wells's name, and Harvard still awards a Wells prize for the best doctoral dissertation.

15

CHARLES L. RICHARDS

T his Norwich native left home for the allure and romance of the gold
mines and the South Seas but returned home to marry and start a
second career.

CHARLES LEWIS RICHARDS

70/248 Broadway

It took only one look for Charles Richards to decide Ada Louise Pollard
would be his wife. He saw her walking along Broadway and told his
companion, "I'm going to marry her."

Richards was born on August 26, 1831, the son of Charles and Emily
(Jerome) Richards. After completing his education, he traveled to the
Sandwich Islands, where he opened a ship's chandlery. When gold was
discovered in California in 1849, he returned to the mainland and ran a
packet boat line between San Francisco and Honolulu.

He returned to Norwich in 1867, bought the house at 70 Broadway and
became a real estate investor. In 1868, Richards married Ada Louise Pollard,
the daughter of Norwich native Elizabeth Potter (Moore) and Uriah Pollard,
an art importer with locations in New York City and New Orleans. Both
of her parents had died, and Ada had been living with her aunt Mary Ann

The Charles L. Richards house at 248 Broadway is now the site of St. Mark's Lutheran Church. *Courtesy of Diane Norman*.

Left: Ship's chandler Charles L. Richards settled in Norwich after living in the Sandwich Islands and Hawaii. *Courtesy of Diane Norman*. *Right*: Ada Louise Pollard married Charles Richards in 1868. *Courtesy of Diane Norman*.

(Moore) and uncle Gurdon Chapman at 269 Broadway in Norwich. The couple had six children. For what may have been a wedding trip, they visited the Sandwich Islands, returning to Norwich about four months before their son Charles was born.

In the 1870 census, Charles Richards was a retired merchant with holdings of $125,000, about $33 million[©] in 2012. Among his projects was the Richards Building on Main Street, which more recently housed Allyn's Bridal Shop.

In 1883, the youngest child, Halsey, was born on September 5. His father died on October 21, leaving Ada a thirty-five-year-old widow with six children, the eldest of whom was fourteen and the youngest only six weeks old. Ada apparently sold the house and rented elsewhere for a few years before returning to her aunt's house in 1890. Mary Chapman died in 1892, and Ada inherited the house.

While she was by all appearances devoted to her family, Mrs. Richards apparently had some outside interests, especially after the children were grown. In 1906, she was a vice-president of United Workers, the city's private social services agency.

Mrs. Richards remained at 269 Broadway until she died in 1922. Her daughter Elizabeth never married and remained in the house until her mother's death, then moved to 93 Sachem Street. Son Charles became a businessman and moved to Chicago. He married Rosalie Decatur Lanman, daughter of Admiral Joseph and Ann Lanman, in 1896 and had five children.

Daughter Ada became the second wife of Albert Chase, son of Daniel H. and Caroline E. (Smith) Chase in 1914. They lived with their daughter and his son from the previous marriage. Albert was president of the Eaton Chase Company hardware store. Louis Richards became a sanitary engineer and moved to Elizabeth, New Jersey, where he lived with his family until his death. Frank Pollard Richards became an accountant and died unmarried in 1955. Halsey settled just outside Newport, Rhode Island, where he was a manufacturer and then a farmer.

16

EDWIN C. AND MRS. "DIAMOND" JOHNSON

H is family ran a mill in Montville. Her father was a wealthy merchant and investor from Chicago. Her signature accessory was diamonds, which she regularly lost.

MRS. "DIAMOND" (MARY) AND EDWIN C. JOHNSON

248 Broadway (1888–1895)

Mary Johnson's background was rock-solid New England, with ancestors dating back to Boston and Salem, Massachusetts, in the 1600s. Her father was a wealthy Chicagoan who saw to it that his daughter had a substantial income of her own. After thirty years of marriage, she tried to divorce her husband; he and their sons called her insane.

Norwich called her Mrs. "Diamond" Johnson for her habit of draping herself with diamonds—which she frequently lost. And that's not to mention her flamboyant lifestyle, the gift of $40,000 in bonds to her coachman and as much as $150,000 in bonds entrusted to her physician—and the lawsuit she filed to recover them.

Mrs. Johnson was born Mary Tuthill King in 1842, the youngest daughter of Tuthill and Susannah (Gates) King of Chicago. A Long Island native,

Tuthill King left home at age twenty and went to Buenos Aires, Argentina, where he was a successful merchant. When he returned to the United States in 1834, he opened a clothing and dry goods store in Chicago and then invested in real estate and made a fortune. He married native Bostonian Susannah Gates, and by the 1860s, the family was living on exclusive Michigan Avenue.

Although it's unknown how they met, nineteen-year-old Mary King married Edwin C. Johnson in 1861 in Norwich. Johnson was the son of William G. Johnson, who was actually wealthier than Tuthill King.

They settled in Montville near Edwin's father, wealthy proprietor of the dye works where Edwin was assistant superintendent and his brother, Charles, superintendent of the plant.

At some point in the mid-1880s, the Johnsons bought the house at 248 Broadway in Norwich, and the city became acquainted with Mrs. Johnson's flamboyancy. The city directory lists Edwin C. Johnson at that address, but later legal proceedings indicate their separation may have begun around that time.

In 1893, Mary Johnson attracted headlines when she lost a pair of valuable earrings during a trip to New York and offered a $2,000 reward for their return. A New London newsboy found the earrings in their chamois bag on the train platform, where they apparently fell while the Johnsons were changing trains. The earrings were said to be four-carat diamonds that had been in Mrs. Johnson's family for some time. The reward was paid after Tiffany, the New York jeweler, confirmed the authenticity of the earrings.

Was she eccentric or mad? Mrs. "Diamond" Johnson laid claim to diamond garters and a custom-built mausoleum. She gave one of her sons $100,000 ($26 million©) as a gift and then changed her mind and hired a lawyer to get the money back. She wasn't pleased when the attorney said there were no grounds for a lawsuit. She had a monument erected in Yantic Cemetery, costing $10,000 ($2.3 million©) or more. After it was completed, she had the vault reinforced to prevent looters from disturbing the grave in hopes of finding jewels. It was said she intended to be buried with her diamonds.

In late 1894, Mrs. Johnson accused her doctor of stealing a large sum of money from the cache of "several thousand dollars" she had hidden about the house. She also alleged he had stolen $150,000 worth of bonds she had given him to keep from her husband. She devised an elaborate plot that involved having the sheriff and others hiding in a dressing room and peering through a peephole in the wall while she received the doctor, intending to entrap him. When that plan fell through, she attached all of the doctor's property and that of his wife and filed a civil suit.

In March 1895, her son Andrew sought to have a conservator appointed for his mother, while she threatened legal proceedings against her husband both for divorce and slander. On her way home from the first day of the probate court hearing, she lost her diamond bracelet.

She alleged her husband had manhandled her in 1892 while they were at New York's famous Fifth Avenue Hotel, striking her arm and threatening her with a gun. She also claimed that a few months later her son Andrew stole items valued at $5,000 from her house. The missing items included dresses, silverware, pictures and sheet music.

She also claimed she married her husband, not from affectionate feeling, but because he swallowed a bottle of laudanum and wouldn't allow his stomach to be pumped until she consented to marry him.

Mrs. Johnson claimed she paid her husband's tailor bills and most of the household expenses and basically dismissed him as a "nobody." She reportedly said that when they married, Edwin Johnson was a "Connecticut woodcutter who didn't own anything but the hair on his head," although his father's holdings were triple those of Tuthill King.

While she sounded quite mad, a long list of Norwich residents were willing to attest to her sanity. The length of the proceedings had obviously begun to try the judge's patience. Contrary to apparent public expectation, the probate ruling went against her, and Dr. Patrick Cassidy was named the conservator. He was able to resign the position after Mrs. Johnson moved to Chicago, effectively putting her beyond the jurisdiction of the Norwich courts. The judge tried to appoint son Fred Johnson to the post, but he declined. It fell to his brother Andrew to post the appropriate bonds. It was expected he would sell the house on Broadway and use the proceeds to pursue a suit in the Illinois courts over her Illinois property.

Andrew Johnson died, however, in 1900, his brother Edwin in 1904 and their father in 1917. Fred Johnson, who had captained a legendary crew team in 1894, graduated from Yale Scientific School in 1894 and then had a successful career in business, running a cotton brokerage under his own name. He served a term in the Connecticut General Assembly in 1911. He married Grace Saltonstall Lee of New York in 1900 and had two children.

Although there reportedly was at least one more try, Mrs. Diamond Johnson apparently never followed through on a divorce action. When she died in Chicago in 1932, Cook County recorded the death of Mary Tuthill King Johnson, whose spouse was Edwin Johnson.

17

THE OSGOODS

A patent medicine to treat malaria led to fame and fortune for this local
physician turned drug manufacturer and wholesaler.

DR. CHARLES OSGOOD (1809–1881)

63/151 Washington Street

Dr. Charles Osgood began his professional life as a physician, but it was as a
drug manufacturer and wholesaler that he was most successful.

Charles Osgood was born in Lebanon, Connecticut, in 1808, one of
seven children of Dr. Erastus Osgood and Martha Morgan. Charles was
educated at Plainfield Academy and then studied with his father for a time
before going to Yale College. After he received his medical diploma in
1833, he studied more medicine in Providence and then moved to Monroe,
Michigan, where he had a large and successful practice.

By 1840, Dr. Osgood had returned to Norwich, and by 1841, his drug
company was in operation. He gained a widespread reputation for patent
medicines like Dr. Osgood's India Cholagogue, which was introduced in the
1840s as a remedy for fever and ague, now generally recognized as malaria.
In 1855, Dr. Osgood wrote a pamphlet, called *The Causes, Treatment, and Cure
of Fever and Ague, and other Diseases of Bilious Climates*, which was included with

The home of drug manufacturer Dr. Charles Osgood at 151 Washington Street was renowned for the tropical plants in the gardens. *Courtesy of the author.*

This fountain, seen at right in the photo of the Osgood house, is now on the Norwich Free Academy campus. *Photo by the author.*

each bottle of medicine. This was patented, and newspaper ads appeared warning against imitations.

In 1839, Dr. Osgood married Sarah Smith Larned and had four children. The drug business grew and made Osgood a wealthy man. As early as 1850, the census shows him reporting real estate valued at $22,135 ($10.3 million©). By the end of the century, the Osgood wealth was nationally recognized, and Charles Osgood was included on a 1902 list of American millionaires published by World Almanac.

As adults, both of Osgood's sons joined their father in the drug manufacturing business. Charles (who identified himself as C. Henry) was listed as a clerk and Frederic a bookkeeper. In 1878, daughter Cornelia married Augustus Cleveland Tyler, son of General Daniel Tyler, who had lived just down Washington Street. Although they moved to the South, they maintained a summer home in New London's Pequot Colony.

Dr. Osgood was very active in the affairs of the city. Besides being an original incorporator of Norwich Free Academy, he was a founder and first president of the Shetucket Bank. His other business involvements included Norwich City Gas Company, New London County Mutual Fire Insurance Company, Norwich Water Power Company and the Norwich Savings Society, as well as a rubber shoe company in Malden, Massachusetts, and a cotton gin company in New London. He was named president of the New London Northern Railroad in 1873.

Politically, the doctor, a Democrat, was said to have little interest in holding office; however, in 1876, he was elected mayor of Norwich, but he resigned for health reasons before completing his term.

Dr. Osgood died in 1881 after a long illness, reportedly leaving one of the largest estates in Norwich.

Fred Osgood married Eliza J. White of New York in 1874. They lived at the corner of Washington and Sachem Streets across from William Blackstone and his wife. Fred Osgood was mayor of Norwich from 1896 to 1900 and listed that as his occupation in the 1900 census. He and Eliza split their time between Norwich and a winter home in New York.

Both sons were yachtsmen, and each owned one of the large private yachts so popular among the wealthy at the time. Charles was at one time commodore of the American Yacht Club. Fred belonged to the New York and Larchmont Yacht Clubs.

C. Henry Osgood had married Anna Alvard by 1880, and they had one child. By 1892, the family had moved to 151 Washington Street. In 1900, C.H. Osgood was still a drug manufacturer and succeeded his father

A uniformed chauffeur drives north on Broadway in a single-cylinder 1902 Packard Model F owned by drug manufacturer C. Henry Osgood. Chelsea Parade is at right, and the Williams mansion (the Teel House) is visible in the background. *Courtesy of Diane Norman.*

as president of the New London Northern Railroad. As well, he was a director of the Hopkins and Allen Company. Anna died in 1912, and Charles apparently remarried, as the 1920 census showed him at seventy-five still living in the family home and married to Jessie Osgood, twenty-five years younger.

GILBERT OSGOOD (1823–1871)

74/270 Broadway

Gilbert Osgood was Dr. Charles Osgood's brother and partner in Charles Osgood & Company. He was born in 1823. In 1854, he married Mary Sanger Backus (1834–1865), daughter of Joseph and Mary (Sanger) Backus, and had four daughters.

Osgood was active in local affairs and was a director of the Shetucket Bank. Politically, he was a Democrat and served on the city's common council. He was one of five voters who filed an injunction against Mayor J. Lloyd Greene to prevent city payment of the bill for powder for a one-hundred-gun cannon salute to mark the Emancipation Proclamation in 1863.

By 1860, the family lived at 74 (now 270) Broadway. Mary Osgood died in 1865 at age thirty-one, leaving her husband with three young daughters. In the 1870 census, the household included Osgood, his daughters, twenty-six-year-old Annette Osgood (presumably a niece or cousin overseeing the household), two domestic servants and a coachman. Osgood reported assets totaling $75,000 ($19.8 million©) and an additional $48,000 ($12 million©) owned by his late wife, apparently held in trust for the girls.

Osgood died in 1871, leaving his daughters orphaned. Mary and Martha went to live with their aunt and uncle Jane (Backus) and Charles Webb on Franklin Street. Five years later, Charles Webb, assistant cashier and president at two local banks, was tried and convicted of embezzlement in a scheme involving two other bank officials. Webb served a five-year prison sentence and returned to Norwich around 1885. Jane Webb died in 1898.

In 1930, Mary and Martha were enumerated at 1 Rockwell Terrace. In the 1940 census, the sisters were still living on Rockwell Terrace, with seventy-four-year-old Martha listed as head of a household that included and eighty-year-old Mary and their cousin Mabel Webb, age sixty-five.

18

J. NEWTON PERKINS

Fortunes won and lost were a hallmark of Newton Perkins's life, both professionally and personally. Along the way, he built a beautiful home and left a lasting legacy for students at Norwich Free Academy.

JOSHUA NEWTON PERKINS (1804–1876)

Pinehurst: 60/154 Washington Street

For many years, Joshua Newton Perkins was considered one of the most influential and honorable members of the New York Stock Exchange. He also was an officer of the Ohio Life Insurance and Trust Company and the Illinois Central Railroad. He came to Norwich about 1850, a wealthy man retired at a relatively young age.

Perkins was born in 1804 in Liverpool, Nova Scotia, the son of John and Elizabeth (Thomas) Perkins. He apparently identified himself as J. Newton or Newton as early as his college days—J. Newton Perkins is listed among the 1826 graduates of Hamilton College in New York.

Perkins lived for some time in Ithaca, New York, where he married Elizabeth Bishop in 1831. Her father, a deacon of the Congregational Church, descended from the Bishop family, which originated in Lisbon, Connecticut. J. Newton and Elizabeth Perkins were the parents of three children.

Financier J. Newton Perkins was among occupants of Pinehurst at 154 Washington Street. *Courtesy of the author.*

Perkins was cashier of the Norwich Bank in 1836 when he left for Cincinnati to become cashier at Ohio Life and Trust Co. A few years later, Perkins moved to New York City, where he became a leading banker and financier. He accumulated a fortune of about $60,000 ($27.9 million[C]), retired to Norwich and built the Italian villa later known as Pinehurst. In 1859, Perkins became a director of the eight-year-old Illinois Central Railroad.

Architect Gervase Wheeler was engaged to design the Perkins house and used painted brick trimmed with Portland stone, set to take advantage of what the architect called a "commanding view" from its bluff overlooking the Yantic River and Hollyhock Island. At the front of the property stood a house formerly owned by William C. Gilman, one of the city's early manufacturers. The Gilman house was moved to a site on Washington Street just north of Chelsea Parade.

Perkins settled into life in his adopted city. Although not an original incorporator, he was a donor after incorporation of the Norwich Free Academy. He established the Newton Perkins Medals, awarded since 1857 to seniors for excellence in Latin, French and artwork and for proficiency in English, chemistry, algebra II, social studies, German and declamation.

Perkins had some financial difficulty around 1860, when the sale of Pinehurst to John F. Slater was recorded, but Perkins nevertheless reported assets totaling $51,000 in the 1860 census. After the loss, Perkins returned to business and established J.N. Perkins & Co. (a brokerage), made a second fortune and apparently was able to reacquire Pinehurst. In the 1870 census, Slater was in his mansion up the hill, and Perkins and his daughter were living at Pinehurst. His occupation was broker, and his real estate holdings had increased.

Disaster struck again a few months later as J.N. Perkins & Co. failed, losing $500,000 ($127 million©). Although Perkins was unable or unwilling to explain the loss, his obituary attributed the failure to Black Friday, the September 24, 1869 crash that occurred as speculators James Fisk and Jay Gould attempted to corner the gold market. When the U.S. government responded by selling $4 million in gold, the price plummeted, and speculators who were unable to sell their holdings were ruined.

For the next few years, Perkins worked for a low salary in an office on Broad Street in New York. Pinehurst was sacrificed after the crash, although it remained empty until after Perkins's death.

About the time his wife died in 1869, Perkins had developed his own health problems. He went to live at his daughter Lucy's home in Irvington-on-Hudson, New York. She had married Edmund Augustus Benedict, a Williams College graduate who was a broker with J.N. Perkins & Co.

Perkins died in 1876, leaving Lucy and her family; his son, Reverend J. Newton Perkins of New York, who had married Emily Soules; and his unmarried daughter Elizabeth, who subsequently left Norwich for Plymouth, Massachusetts.

19

The Nortons

The Norton brothers were born in Branford, Connecticut, the sons of Asa and Sophia (Barker) Norton, whose ancestors reached back to the early settlement of the town. The family included brothers Henry, Timothy and William. Their sister, Emily, married the wealthy merchant and manufacturer Lorenzo Blackstone. All eventually moved to Norwich and went from being grocers to partners with multiple and diverse holdings.

Henry Barker Norton (1807–1891)

70/188 Washington Street

It is said that in 1824, Henry B. Norton came to Norwich with only a dollar in his pocket. True or not, by the time he died sixty-seven years later, he had amassed a considerable fortune and become one of the town's most prominent citizens.

He was born in 1807, and in 1838, Henry married Emeline Frisbie, the daughter of Calvin and Polly (Harrison) Frisbie of Branford. Three of their seven children, including the only son, died in childhood.

Norton's business career began in 1827, when nineteen-year-old Henry Norton and Joseph Backus began a partnership as merchants. Over the years, Henry Norton considerably expanded his business interests. He was

Above: Merchant and industrialist Henry B. Norton and his family lived in the Greek Revival house at 188 Washington Street. *Photo by the author.*

Left: Henry B. Norton. *Courtesy of Slater Memorial Museum.*

president of the Norwich & New London Steamboat Company, and in 1848, the Norton brothers bought three steamboats, which were apparently put into service by the company to run in conjunction with the railroad.

Profits must have been very good from the start. The Nortons were living at 188 Washington Street as early as October 1845, when a fire was reported in the charcoal that had been delivered for heating the house. The fire was extinguished before any damage was done.

H.B. Norton was among the wealthy Norwich residents recruited to establish Norwich Free Academy. He was an original incorporator and later served as president of the trustees. Norton was a director of the New London, Willimantic & Palmer Railroad and Norwich Bleaching, Dyeing and Calendaring Company. Additionally, he owned wharf space in the harbor and owned or had shares in several ships.

In addition, Norton was involved in banking and manufacturing. He was an organizer of the Uncas and Chelsea Savings Banks, and in 1859, he became president of the Attawaugan Company, which employed about five hundred hands making fine cotton cloth. The mill ownership was a partnership that included his brother William and brother-in-law Lorenzo Blackstone.

During the Civil War, Norton worked closely with Governor Buckingham to procure whatever was needed for the troops, from transportation to supplies, and "attended personally to the wants and comforts of our men in the field." In *The Norwich Memorial: Annals of Norwich in the Great Rebellion*, Reverend Malcolm McGregor Dana said of Norton, "Soldiers came to feel that if he was on the look-out for them, they would not suffer for the lack of anything his thoughtful care and means could provide." Dana noted that Norton declined all commissions and refused every offer of compensation. When Governor Buckingham died in 1875, H.B. Norton was a pallbearer in the funeral procession and identified in the newspapers as a close friend of the governor.

Like many others, Norton's fortune increased dramatically during the 1860s. In the 1860 census, he reported real estate and personal holdings of $46,000. In 1870, his reported holdings totaled $270,000 ($63.4 million©). Ten years later, at seventy-three, Norton was still identified as a manufacturer in the 1880 census. Emeline and the three girls were still in the household, and the staff remained at two.

Prior to his death in 1891, he had contributed funds for an art gallery adjacent to the Slater Memorial Museum. Norton's will included a $50,000 bequest for NFA. Besides the bequest to NFA, Norton left $200,000 to the Norwich Public Library and Reading Room; $15,000 to Broadway Congregational Church; and $5,000 each to United Workers (now United Community Services) and the Eliza Huntington Home, with additional bequests to the Norwich YMCA, American Seamen's Friends Society, American Home Missionary Society, American Board of Commissioners of Foreign Missions and American Congregational Missions.

Daughter Emeline never married. Her twin sister Isabella Farnsworth married Lorenzo Blackstone's brother, Timothy Beach Blackstone, in 1868 and moved to Chicago. Mary and Ella died unmarried and remained at 188 Washington Street until well into the twentieth century.

WILLIAM T. NORTON (1826–1871)

71/263 Broadway

William Tyler Norton had everything going for him when, at age forty-four, his life was suddenly cut short in a steamboat fire as he stayed to help others before finally leaving the ship.

He was born in 1826, and like his brothers, William moved to Norwich and joined the family grocery business. As they accumulated capital, the Nortons expanded their interests and formed partnerships with other Norwich businessmen. For example, in 1848, Norton, Converse & Co. bought the steamboats *Knickerbocker*, *Worcester* and *Cleopatra*.

The Norton business was profitable enough that the 1865 tax list put his annual income at $20,000 ($7.43 million©).

More opportunities for diversification arose for William and his brothers in the 1850s when their sister, Emily, and her husband, Lorenzo Blackstone, moved to Norwich from England, where Lorenzo had become quite wealthy as a rubber goods merchant.

In partnership with the Norton brothers, Lorenzo Blackstone and his son DeTrafford bought the Hooper Mill. Blackstone later incorporated the Attawaugan Company in 1872 as the parent corporation for all of their mills.

Although his name seldom appeared in connection with civic affairs, William Norton was listed as a member of the committee for the city's bicentennial ball in 1859.

William returned to Branford in November 1852 to marry Mary Elizabeth Plant, and they had three children.

William T. Norton died in a steamboat explosion nine years after moving to this house at 263 Broadway. *Photo by the author.*

About 1863, after many years on Church Street, Norton moved his family to a house on Broadway at the corner of Rockwell Street. With the move, his family was surrounded by fashionable and wealthy Norwich citizens—Lucius Carroll lived on the other corner and General and Mrs. Williams just up the street. His brother Henry's house on Washington Street was a short walk.

W.T. Norton was among seven passengers returning to Norwich from New York aboard the steamboat *City of New London* on November 21, 1871. Typically, the boats left New York and steamed up Long Island Sound during the night, arriving at Norwich the next morning after a stop in New London.

About 4:00 a.m. on November 22, the boat anchored off Montville because a snow squall impaired visibility. As the cook was making breakfast, he apparently laid a red-hot poker near a partition, where it ignited the woodwork. The crew extinguished the blaze, and the boat got underway; however, around 6:00 a.m., a second fire broke out. Apparently a spark from the earlier fire landed on cotton bales piled near the kitchen door and smoldered until breaking into flames.

Access to life preservers was blocked by the fire, and passengers were forced into the icy water. Norton's heroism was noted by witnesses at the later hearing. They testified that Norton assisted others, including the sole female passenger, before he left the flaming vessel.

Also aboard were Norwich merchant Henry K. Hammond and manufacturer Caleb B. Rogers. Hammond, who jumped off the bow with Norton, was rescued. Although he was near death, Hammond directed rescuers to the opposite side of the boat to look for Norton, but they were unable to find him. Rogers was among the sixteen passengers and crew who also perished.

Norton's body was not immediately found. Henry and Timothy Norton put up a $1,000 reward for recovery of their brother's body, but it was not until January 1872 that the papers reported William's body had been found by a young girl in Groton, fifteen miles to the south.

The widowed Mary Norton remained in the Broadway house. Daughter Angelina married Edward Fuller, a commission grocer in 1876, and had four children. After her mother's death in 1879, Angelina and her husband apparently continued the Norton household. In 1930, the Fullers' daughter, Angelina, was still at 263 (previously 71) Broadway. Son Henry, who married in 1884 and was divorced by 1920, lived at various boardinghouses. Young William married Martha W. Brewer and had four children. By 1905, William was secretary of the Edward Chappell Company, his wife's family's firm. After her husband's death, Martha and their daughter Ruth remained at 227 Broadway.

Timothy Parmelee Norton (1816–1877)

38 Washington Street

Timothy P. Norton, who was born in 1816, was the low-profile Norton brother about whom little was written but who was, nevertheless, a respected member of the Norwich community.

For many years, in addition to being a wholesale grocer, T.P. Norton was a director of the Norwich Fire Insurance Company, a director of Bacon Manufacturing Company and of both the Farmers' and Mechanics' and Thames National Banks. In 1839, his name appeared on the rolls of the Apollo Association for the Promotion of the Fine Arts in the United States.

When the Civil War began, T.P. Norton was named a vice-president of the permanent committee established to oversee Norwich's war effort.

Although not an original incorporator of Norwich Free Academy, T.P. Norton was listed as a donor after incorporation.

In 1842, Norton married Jane Denison Tyler, daughter of Reverend John Tyler, longtime rector of Christ Episcopal Church. The Nortons' house was next door to the church.

Jane Tyler died at age thirty-six in 1855, leaving her husband a widower with an eleven-year-old son. The 1860 census showed her husband, a housekeeper, a maid and son Frank (then sixteen) still living on Washington Street.

Like many others, T.P. Norton became a very wealthy man between 1860 and 1870. His holdings went from $30,000 in 1860 to $250,000 in 1870 ($66 million© today). Tax assessment lists in the 1860s put his annual income at $17,230 ($3.21 million©).

Frank Norton graduated valedictorian of his class at Trinity College in 1868 and went to Europe for a year before entering the Berkeley Divinity School in Middletown, Connecticut. He was ordained in 1872, and his first assignment was St. Thomas Church in New York. In 1877, he was profiled in an article about St. Thomas in *Frank Leslie's Weekly Sunday Magazine*. By 1880, Reverend Norton, thirty-four, was living in Troy with his wife and three children. From there they went to Massachusetts, where Reverend Norton died in Boston in 1891.

20

CHARLES A. CONVERSE

In Norwich, Charles Converse is mainly remembered for the manufacture of pistols, the art gallery that bears his name at the Slater Memorial Museum and his distinctive Gothic-style home.

CHARLES AUGUSTUS CONVERSE (1815–1901)

77/185 Washington Street

Charles A. Converse was born in 1815 in Salem, Massachusetts, the son of Augustus and Amy Hyde (Mansfield). The family came to Norwich in 1834. In 1845, Charles Converse married Caroline Frances Balcam, the daughter of Socrates and Amy (Bingham) Balcam of Windham, and had two children.

Converse was a merchant, manufacturer and, at one time, a division inspector of militia with the rank of lieutenant colonel, so he was called Colonel Converse. He was an original director of Shetucket (later National) Bank when it was organized in 1853, a member of the Norwich Board of Education and also a director of the Norwich Library Association.

He chaired the executive general committee that oversaw planning for an 1868 visit by New York's Seventh Regiment. The daylong extravaganza included plenty of marching and maneuvering, a gala luncheon and speaking program and an evening ball.

Firearms manufacturer Colonel Charles A. Converse built this house at 185 Washington Street around 1870. *Courtesy of Slater Memorial Museum.*

He was initially a hardware merchant, but in 1865, Colonel Converse constructed a building formally known as the Falls Commonwealth Works. His tenants included factories that produced woolen cloth, nails, flour and files; a cork-cutting factory; and a dye works. There were also four firearms manufacturers, including Ethan Allen & Thurber, Norwich Falls Pistol, T&K Bacon and Hopkins & Allen.

Colonel Converse was the largest shareholder of the Bacons' company, and when he became unhappy with the firm's management, he took over the company. The new firm kept the Bacon Manufacturing name for a time, but eventually, Converse and some former Bacon employees formed Hopkins & Allen, operating on the former Bacon premises.

They manufactured shotguns, rifles and inexpensive handguns, and Hopkins & Allen became the third-largest gun maker in the country. Only Samuel Colt's company in Hartford and Winchester Arms in New Haven were bigger.

In 1874, Colonel Converse sold his interest in Hopkins & Allen and, within a year, became secretary of the Hood Firearms Company, which operated about four years.

Charles Converse was listed in the 1850 census with Caroline, the two children and two servants. His occupation was hardware merchant with no financial information listed. They lived on Crescent Street in a house that was later torn down to expand the Norwich Free Academy campus.

In 1860, Colonel Converse was a manufacturer with $56,000 in assets. By 1870, his holdings had increased to $110,000 ($29 million©).

Daughter Caroline, who was called Carrie, married Alfred E. Austin, a lawyer from South Norwalk, Connecticut, and had a daughter. Edward married Alice Sterry in 1876, and they were still living with his parents in 1880. The occupation given for both father and son is pistol manufacturer.

Although not an original incorporator of Norwich Free Academy, Colonel Converse was listed as a donor after incorporation, and he later funded an art gallery addition to the Slater Museum. The Converse Gallery opened in 1906, five years after his death.

21

Colonel George L. Perkins

Colonel George L. Perkins once walked from Norwich to Poughkeepsie, New York, to ride on Robert Fulton's steamboat as it traveled down the Hudson River to New York City. He had been a paymaster in the War of 1812; fifty years later, at age eighty-three, he was a dispatch courier traveling through hostile territory to reach President Lincoln early in the Civil War. And he lived to be exactly one hundred years, one month old.

Colonel George Leonard Perkins (1788–1888)

57 Broadway (Site of St. Patrick Cathedral Property)

George Leonard Perkins was an extraordinary man who was born in Norwich on August 5, 1788, the son of Hezekiah and Sarah (Fitch) Perkins. As a young man, he was considered consumptive, so at twenty-two, he took an ocean voyage, hoping to gain good health. He was feeble and had to be carried off the ship when it reached Brazil, but after a few months in the tropics and a return voyage, he arrived home in robust health.

Back in Norwich, Perkins became a merchant, but by 1812, the United States was at war with Great Britain, and Perkins was appointed paymaster for the second district, covering Connecticut and Rhode Island. He was present at the

Colonel George L. Perkins, for fifty years treasurer of the Norwich & Worcester Railroad, lived to be one hundred years old. *Courtesy of the author.*

bombardment of Stonington in 1814. Until the end of his life, he was known as Colonel Perkins.

After the war, he returned to business and, in 1819, married Emily Lathrop. They had four children, two of whom died young. Between them, they had ties to most of Norwich's founding families.

The Perkins' estate, called Maplewood, extended up Broadway to Charles Johnson's house. After construction of St. Patrick Church began in 1870, the family moved around the corner to the new Perkins Place (now Avenue), and the portion of the estate grounds nearest Broadway became the school and rectory.

Colonel Perkins was an original incorporator and director of the Norwich & Worcester Railroad. He was the railroad's first treasurer and served fifty-three years, still going to the office at age ninety-eight. On his 100th birthday, he was hailed as the oldest living railroad man in the United States.

He also was an original incorporator of the Norwich Savings Society and director of the First National Bank. When it was organized, he transferred his church membership to Park Congregational Church and established its first Sunday school. Although not an incorporator, Colonel Perkins was among the donors after incorporation of Norwich Free Academy.

He prided himself on having voted in every presidential election since James Madison. Perkins had met a half dozen presidents who made a point of calling on him while visiting Norwich. He noted he'd never met Grover Cleveland, although he'd known the president's grandfather well.

He was a witness in the 1875 Beecher-Tilton "Trial of the Century," in which noted clergyman Henry Ward Beecher was accused of adultery with a member of his congregation. Colonel Perkins testified he saw Reverend

Beecher on a train in Worcester on the same date the plaintiff said the minister was in New York.

Contemporaries described Colonel Perkins as a six-foot-, two-inch-tall, active but not athletic man who had a military carriage and always dressed in black and white. He was a favored partner at balls, as he was a "good waltzer." He also had a whimsical sense of humor, evidenced in a scene that occurred one day when he was in his nineties. He was with a group of children listening to an organ grinder. He said he "danced them a hornpipe and I think they enjoyed it," he told an interviewer.

To mark Colonel Perkins's 100th birthday in 1888, more than 1,500 people crowded into Norwich's Arcanum Club, and he shook hands with each one. The crowd included not only Norwich friends and neighbors but also railroad officials and statesmen from afar. A few days later, he addressed a visiting firemen's association, which hailed him as the oldest living fireman in the world.

Colonel Perkins died on September 5, 1888, just a month after his birthday, while the family was on their annual vacation at Fort Griswold House, the Groton seaside resort. His ninety-year-old widow, Emily, and daughter, Emily, lived on Perkins Place (now Perkins Avenue) until the mother's death. In the 1900 census, sixty-three-year-old Emily Perkins, who never married, was boarding with the Misses Meeker at 130 Washington Street.

Their son, Thomas H. Perkins, married Elizabeth Lusk in 1862 and had a son who lived only a year. After Elizabeth's death in 1870, Thomas married Helen Reynolds, the daughter of steamboat Captain Charles and Helen M. Reynolds, and with her had four children. Helen's sister Mary Day Reynolds was married to Senator (formerly governor) Buckingham's nephew William.

22

MOSES PIERCE

His businesses employed two thousand people with an annual payroll estimated at $1 million. He lived in southern New England, but his name is on a dormitory at the Hampton Institute in Virginia.

MOSES PIERCE (1808–1900)

6/24 Broad Street and 274 Broadway

Moses Pierce was born in 1808 in Pawtucket, Rhode Island, the son of Benjamin B. and Susan (Walker) Pierce. At age fourteen, he left school to work in a mill. A few years later, he went into accounting, and by age twenty-nine, he was assigned to manage a mill in Willimantic, Connecticut.

Harriet Hathaway, daughter of Simmons and Harriet (Gardner) Hathaway, became his wife in 1831, and they had five children. One son died in childhood and another at age twenty-eight.

Pierce came to Norwich in 1840 at the invitation of Norwich mill owner Jedidiah Leavens to establish a bleachery in Greeneville. Under his leadership, Norwich Bleaching, Calendaring & Dyeing grew from a dozen to more than four hundred hands, becoming one of the largest textile finishing operations in the nation.

Moses Pierce lived in this house at 24 Broad Street. It was later the home of Ellen Young Peck, William A. Slater's mother-in-law. *Photo by the author.*

Pierce became a director of the Norwich & Worcester Railroad and also of the Second National and Chelsea Savings banks. He was president of the Norwich & New York Transportation Company for eleven years. Pierce saw the need for water rights along the Shetucket River and was instrumental in acquiring those rights and organizing the Occum Water Power Company in the early 1860s. That move allowed establishment of the textile mill in Taftville that became the Ponemah Mill, which claimed to be the largest cotton mill under one roof in the world.

Pierce's wealth didn't grow as quickly as others' did between 1860 and 1870. He had accumulated assets of $17,000 in 1860, and ten years later, that had increased to $62,000 ($16.4 million[©]). In later years, however, his wealth grew to very substantial amounts.

He became president and treasurer of Norwich Bleaching, Calendaring & Dyeing Company, which eventually became U.S. Finishing Co. He was also president of the Ashland and Aspinook mills in Jewett City. At his death, the total employment at his companies was estimated at two thousand people and the annual combined payroll at no less than $1 million.

For some years, the Pierce family lived in the former Jessie Brown Tavern on the Norwich Town Green. In 1873, Pierce donated the house to be used as an orphanage and moved his family to 6 (now 24) Broad Street. It is unknown whether this was a response to Harriet's death in 1870, a desire to move to a more fashionable section of town or recognition of a need by a man who had the financial wherewithal to do something about it. Regardless of the motive, the family lived on Broad Street for about sixteen years and then moved to 276 Broadway, which had been the home of Marianna (Mrs. John) Slater until her death in 1889. It is now the residence of the Roman Catholic bishop of Norwich.

In 1886, Moses Pierce married a second time to Anna E. Holbrook in Malden, Massachusetts.

Pierce had a great interest in education. He was an original incorporator of Norwich Free Academy and served as a trustee there and also at Hampton Institute in Virginia. In 1893, he donated funds for a machine shop for students of Hampton's Trade School. That building is now the Moses Pierce Honors Residence Hall for incoming presidential and trustee scholars.

Pierce was vice-president of the American Society of Inventors, a fellow of the American Geographical Society, a member of the Metropolitan Museum in New York and a member of textile manufacturing trade associations. He made eight trips to Europe, at least one of which was with his friend John F. Slater.

When he died in 1900, Pierce's will stipulated that the income from $100,000 ($18.9 million©) worth of bonds be split between his daughters and, after their deaths, the money be used to establish the Edwin Milman Pierce Fund, specifically for training industrial arts teachers for the common schools serving the African American population in the South.

Income from a second $100,000 block of stock was also split between his daughters during their lifetimes and then divided into ten parts, with six to Norwich Free Academy for its Industrial Arts Department and the rest to establish an orphanage in Pawtucket. He also left about $20,000 in securities for operation of the Rock Nook Home, the orphanage founded at his former residence.

Harriet Pierce never married and remained at 276 Broadway until her death in 1910. Her sister, Emily, married Thomas Wattles and had one child, who died before 1900. They lived on East Town Street until Harriet's death and then moved to Broadway. Emily died in 1915 and Wattles in 1921.

23

Amos W. Prentice

When a town meeting promised to be raucous, Amos Prentice was the man they wanted chairing the meeting. His counsel had been so valuable to directors of an insurance company that when he resigned, they personally delivered a token of their esteem.

Amos Wylie Prentice

83/305 Broadway

A.W. Prentice began as a clerk, succeeded the Breed brothers as owner of their hardware store and ropewalk and became a recognized leader in the community. As longtime trustee of Norwich Free Academy, he made a point of attending graduation exercises. His home is now Allis House, the administration building on the NFA campus.

Prentice was born in 1816 in Griswold, the son of Amos and Lucy (Wylie) Prentice, with lineage extending back to the earliest days of the country. After his father's death, young Amos was sent to Norwich to live with an uncle. He clerked in William Buckingham's store, then went to work in the hardware store owned by the Breed brothers and, by 1840, became a partner.

In 1840, Prentice married Hannah E. Parker, the daughter of Elias and Grace (Mansfield) Parker of Middletown. Two of their children grew to

Hardware merchant A.W. Prentice lived for many years at 305 Broadway. The house is now the administrative office building at Norwich Free Academy. *Photo by the author.*

adulthood. Daughter Mary T. Prentice married Francis Dorrance and had one son. Her sister, Anna, married Albert Chase and was the mother of four children.

In 1864, the firm became A.W. Prentice & Co. and operated under that name until Prentice retired in 1889. It then became the Eaton Chase Company to reflect the ownership of a partner and Prentice's son-in-law Albert Chase.

Prentice was drawn to politics and public affairs. A Republican, he was mayor of Norwich from 1858 to 1860, served in the state legislature in 1877 and served on Norwich's Common Council for ten years. A contemporary biographer suggested the man never sought the office; rather, the office sought the man. Prentice was reportedly the first man in New England to propose the name of Abraham Lincoln as president. During the Civil War, it was Amos Prentice who almost invariably presided over town meetings called to devise ways to help the soldiers and the Union. Prentice was a friend and advisor to Governor Buckingham.

A longtime director of the Norwich Savings Society, Prentice became the bank's president in 1890. In addition, he was a director of First National

Bank and the Richmond Stove Company. He was a deacon of the Broadway Congregational Church, which he had been active in establishing.

Prentice was for many years a director of the Norwich Fire Insurance Company. His counsel was so valued that when he left the board, the remaining members went to his home to make a formal presentation of a "service of plate," probably a silver tea service with a tray, teapot and related flatware. Such a presentation was a mark of esteem for the recipient.

When he died in 1894, Prentice was described as "easily the ideal citizen of Norwich. He was the soul of honor and enjoyed the full confidence of the people of this vicinity. He possessed a broad mind and a kindly disposition and was charitable to all in need."

24

The Smiths and the Mowrys

D avid Smith's company made the paper for national publications such as *Harper's Weekly*. His son-in-law, James Mowry, made his mark as a maker of firearms during the Civil War.

David Smith (1796–1873)

72/256 Broadway (Site of St. Mark's Lutheran Church)

In the world of paper manufacturing, David Smith, head of Chelsea Manufacturing Company, was a superstar. He produced the paper for the most widely read publication in the country on the largest paper mill in the United States, if not the world.

Smith was born in Norwich in 1796, but his career as a papermaker began in nearby Willimantic. By 1833, he was recruited to come to Norwich to assume operation of the Chelsea Manufacturing Company in Greeneville. Under his leadership, the company grew until Chelsea employed about two hundred people and, with a 375-foot main building, claimed to be the largest papermaking operation in the world.

The mill produced high-grade paper for books as well as a coated stock for printing the Harper & Brothers' publications—*Harper's Weekly*, *Harper's Monthly* and *Harper's Bazaar*. *Harper's Weekly* was the most widely read journal

David Smith was president of Chelsea Manufacturing Company, which produced coated stock for the Collier group's magazines. *Courtesy of David Oat.*

in America during the Civil War. Smith's main partner in the venture was J.S. Rives, former publisher of the *Congressional Globe* in Washington, D.C. The company's annual production was estimated at $475,000.

In 1822, Smith went to Windham to marry Lucy Curtis. They later had a daughter.

The Smiths lived in Greeneville until 1856, when they moved to 72 (256) Broadway. Smith's 1864 annual income was reported to be $13,331 ($2.47 million©).

By 1870, daughter Emily Louisa (E. Louisa) had married James D. Mowry, and the couple and their four children were living with the Smiths.

Smith was an original incorporator of Norwich Free Academy and generous supporter of the Congregational Church. In 1864, he was one of the incorporators of the new Second National Bank and was its second president. He also was a vice-president of Chelsea Bank and, for about twenty years, president of Jewett City Savings Bank. As well, he was a director of the Norwich Water Power Company and helped establish the Norwich & New York Transportation Company, serving as its second president. Additionally, he was a director of the two local railroads. Although he generally avoided politics, he served a single one-year term as state senator from Norwich.

Lucy Smith died on July 20, 1873. David Smith survived her by only a few months, dying on November 7, 1873.

James Dixon Mowry (1821–1895)

72/256 Broadway

James Dixon Mowry was perhaps best known for the weapons he manufactured during the Civil War. His guns were variously produced under the J.D. Mowry label, Norwich Arms Company and in conjunction with A.H. Almy's Eagle Manufacturing Company.

Mowry was born in 1820 in Canterbury, the son of Samuel and Cynthia (Cary) Mowry. As a young man, James was employed at his father's very successful machine shop in Greeneville. Samuel Mowry appeared on an 1865 list of the city's wealthiest men with a yearly income in excess of $12,000 ($2.19 million©).

James Mowry married Emily Louisa Smith in 1844 and had four children. The young Mowrys lived in Greeneville with Emily's parents for some years after their marriage. By 1860, they were living at 62 Broadway, just down the street from Emily's parents. Like his father-in-law, Mowry was an original director of Second National Bank when it was organized in 1864 and served as its first cashier. Mowry worked as an agent of Chelsea Manufacturing Company and the Rockland mill before becoming a firearms manufacturer during the Civil War.

In 1862, with some help from Senator Lafayette Foster, a Norwich neighbor, Mowry landed a contract to provide thirty thousand Springfield rifles for the army. No place in town was big enough to do the work, so the barrels were made at the Cole & Walker machine shop on Willow Street, the locks at C.B. Rogers & Coin East Great Plain and the rest at the Mowry machine shop in Greeneville. A.H. Almy, meanwhile, had acquired a contract of his own for Eagle Manufacturing to produce twenty-five thousand muskets. For the next year, they frantically worked at the facilities of both companies to produce muskets and bayonets for Union soldiers.

In 1863, they apparently decided to consolidate, and Mowry and Almy were among the six incorporators of Norwich Arms Company. Almy was president of the company and Mowry its general agent. Their 1864 government contract was for fifteen thousand Springfield rifle muskets at $19.50 apiece. That contract, worth $28,500, would be the last, both because the war was winding down and because the muzzleloader technology had become outdated. By 1866, the Norwich Arms Company was out of business.

After the war, the Mowrys were connected with William H. Page's Wood Type Company and later the Page Steam Heating Company. The wooden type company was the main producer of wooden printing type in the nation. Among their typeface designs was Tuscan No. 9, which was ubiquitous in advertising of the era.

The Mowry Axle Company invented a brake for railroad cars and recovered a substantial settlement in an 1874 patent-infringement case. Railroads had been using the brakes without paying any royalties, so the U.S. Circuit Court in Chicago ruled that Mowry was owed more than $63,000 ($16.9 million©).

In the 1870 census, James and E. Louisa (as she was then calling herself) were enumerated with her parents and a single servant. James's occupation was spring and axe handle manufacturer. Their son David, at twenty-four, was also listed as an axe handle manufacturer,

Son William Mowry was treasurer of the Page Steam Heating Company, and in the late 1880s, he served as an aide on the governor's staff and as a member of the general assembly. In 1894, he was elected Connecticut's secretary of state with the highest total vote among the candidates on the ticket. The Norwich City Directory continued to show his address as 256 Broadway and his occupation as manufacturer, but in Hartford, he is listed with an office at the capitol. He died unmarried in 1898. In 1891, Louisa married Frederick T. Mason, a clerk and then bookkeeper at the Norwich Savings Society, and had a daughter. They lived in Norwich for a time and then moved to Pequot Avenue in New London.

25

THE CHARLES JOHNSON FAMILY

Charles Johnson had a reputation for helping others. When he commissioned portraits of prominent men, he not only helped the artist but also left a legacy for posterity.

CHARLES JOHNSON (1806–1879)

61/227 Broadway

Charles Johnson was a longtime banker in Norwich, but his career began in factories, as a mill hand at age fourteen, then in the company store and, finally, in the office as an accountant and bookkeeper.

Johnson was born in Jewett City in 1806, the son of John and Lydia Johnson. For a few years, he ran a store with his father and then came to Norwich and opened Cobb & Johnson at the Norwich Falls.

He married Hannah Morgan Coit on March 9, 1830. Their son, Charles Coit Johnson (1831), was the only one of Johnson's children to reach adulthood. Hannah Johnson died on July 11, leaving her husband a widower with a four-month-old baby. On October 11, 1836, Johnson married Mary Ann Lester, the daughter of a sea captain. Their daughter, Mary Ann, was born on October 2, 1839, and her mother died nine days later, three years to the day after her marriage. Young Mary Ann died in 1869. Charles Johnson married for the third time in 1850. His bride, Mary Mulligan—the daughter of a New York minister—had a daughter, Mary Mulligan Johnson, in 1864. The mother died seventeen days after the baby's birth, once again leaving Johnson a widower with an infant.

In 1831, Johnson was appointed cashier of the newly organized Jewett City Bank at a salary of $200 annually. When J. Newton Perkins left Norwich Bank to become treasurer of Ohio Life and Trust, the bank sought out Johnson to replace him at a five-fold increase in salary. In 1847, Johnson was named president of Norwich Bank and held that position until his death.

During his early years in Norwich, the new Norwich Savings Society was in the same building as Norwich Bank, and Johnson helped the Savings Society get off the ground. He became a director and trustee in about 1840 and then president of the Savings Society in 1865. During his tenure as president, deposits at the Savings Society increased from less than $150,000 to nearly $8 million.

While Savings Society president, Johnson commissioned Norwich artist Alexander Emmons to paint portraits of thirty "Norwich Worthies"—the city's prominent men. The actual number of portraits totaled thirty-one, including a portrait of the janitor at Johnson's bank, whom he deemed as equally worthy as the other subjects. When Charles Johnson and his brother Frank were designing a new bank building, they included studio space for Emmons. The portraits originally hung in Otis Library but were later given to the Slater Museum for display.

Johnson administered public and private trusts and conducted a brokerage house. He was the first treasurer of the Otis Library and also was treasurer of the local fund for the benefit of soldiers' families during the Civil War. Additionally, Johnson was a director of the Norwich & Worcester Railroad. He had been appointed a trustee of the Southern Minnesota Railroad and was assisting in its reorganization when he died. This involved marketing about $6 million worth of bonds, some of which were sold locally, and they had begun to recover their original price.

Johnson was an organizer and original director of the Norwich City Gas Company and a director of the Norwich Fire Insurance Company, serving as president from 1846 to 1851. He was an original incorporator of Norwich Free Academy and belonged to Park Congregational Church. He was also a benefactor to many causes. It was said that during his lifetime, he quietly donated nearly $150,000 to various religious and benevolent enterprises.

While not a politician, he was interested in politics and enjoyed a good political discussion. Johnson greatly admired Daniel Webster, enough to travel to Marshfield, Massachusetts, to attend Webster's funeral in 1852. He was a strong abolitionist and, later, an active supporter of the Union cause during the war.

Johnson died in April 1879, having survived three wives and two of his three children.

CHARLES COIT JOHNSON (1831–1899)

67/249 Broadway

Although his father may have been a prominent Norwich banker, Charles C. Johnson was well known in his own right as treasurer of the steamboat company and then president of the Norwich City Gas Company.

Charles Coit Johnson was born in Jewett City in 1831. By the time he was nineteen, his mother had died, and he lived with his father in a boardinghouse. At twenty-seven, he reported his occupation as "clerk."

C.C. Johnson, first president of the Norwich Gas & Electric Company, lived at 249 Broadway. The house is being renovated after a 2012 fire. *Photo by the author.*

Charles Coit Johnson received a presidential appointment as allotment commissioner for the Connecticut State Troops in 1862. During the war, three commissioners were appointed for each state to visit the troops in the field and offer arrangements to send a portion of their pay—an allotment—to their families at home.

In 1863, Charles C. Johnson married Julia Cleveland White, the daughter of Norman and Mary Abediah (Dodge) White, a paper manufacturer who was also connected with his father's manufacturing chemists firm Charles T. White & Co. of New York. Julia's sister Emma was married to prominent physician Benjamin Lee, son of the Right Reverend Alfred Lee, first Episcopal bishop of Delaware and a Norwich native. Three of their five children died in childhood.

By 1880, Charles had become treasurer of the Norwich City Gas Company. Later, the company became the Gas and Electric Light Company, precursor of today's Norwich Department of Public Utilities, and C.C. Johnson was president of the combined firm.

Julia Johnson died in 1893. Charles survived her by six years, dying in 1899. Daughter Elsie married John Marbury Reynolds in 1902 and moved to Philadelphia, where they lived with their daughter.

Son Frederick Morgan Johnson graduated from Yale in 1891 and moved to New York, where he married Janet Posey Smith in Pelham Manor in 1903. They had no children. Fred worked for the Brooklyn Telephone Company and a bank for a few years before joining New York Life Insurance Company. He became secretary of the corporation in 1927. He died three years after retiring in 1941.

26

THE ERASTUS WILLIAMS FAMILY

W hen Captain Erastus Williams came to Norwich, he settled on Broadway, but it was in the village of Yantic that his family had the greatest impact.

CAPTAIN ERASTUS WILLIAMS (1793–1867)

70 Broadway

Erastus Williams was born in 1793 in Essex, Connecticut. He went to sea at an early age and made a small fortune as a ship's master (captain). He retired and came to Norwich, where, after the death of his first wife, he married Elizabeth Dorr Tracy in 1829 and had two children.

Captain Williams acquired a parcel of land in northern Norwich known as West Farm and renamed it Yantic, from an Indian name meaning "Little River." He built the Yantic Mill, a church, houses for the mill hands and a store. Williams realized the mill would be destroyed if it ever caught fire, so in 1847, he petitioned the Connecticut General Assembly to charter a village fire company, which became Yantic Fire Engine Company No. 1.

Captain Williams and his wife reared their family in the Broadway house later owned by Charles Richards. After his marriage, son E. Winslow lived nearby. Daughter Elizabeth married John Taylor Huntington, a wealthy

This Tudor-style firehouse was built by E. Winslow Williams to house Yantic Fire Engine Company No. 1. *Photo by the author.*

clergyman and professor of Greek at Trinity College in Hartford, and had four children.

By the 1850 census, Erastus Williams reported $30,000 real estate ($13.6 million©). He was an original donor and incorporator of Norwich Free Academy.

The Williams holdings were not limited to the factory and buildings in Yantic. Captain Williams was the owner of the Merchants' Hotel on Main Street. In 1867, Winslow Williams built a brick building next door and then renovated the hotel, giving it a new façade to match the new building, which housed a dry goods store. Williams was also the first president of the Norwich Bleaching, Calendaring & Dyeing Company.

Elizabeth Tracy Williams died in 1855. Captain Williams, surviving his wife by nearly twelve years, died in 1867.

E. WINSLOW WILLIAMS (1830–1888)

66 Broadway, then Rockclyffe in Yantic

Erastus Winslow Williams was born in Norwich in 1830. Through his mother, he could trace his lineage to original Norwich settlers William Hyde and John Tracy. He graduated from Trinity College, later serving on the school's board of trustees. He married Lydia Marvin McNulty of New York in 1858, and they had four children.

In 1859, Winslow Williams was seeking a tenant for the house at the corner of Broad and Broadway. In the 1860s, it appears that was the family home, clearly identified as owned by E.W. Williams on the 1868 city map.

After college, Winslow came home to run the Yantic Woolen Mill. Despite the foresight and careful planning of his father, a fire destroyed the entire mill on May 26, 1864. Winslow Williams, who by then was leasing the mill from his father, immediately began planning a new building and laid the cornerstone in 1865. The new mill opened on April 16, 1866, when Winslow's sons, Louis, age eight, and Winslow Tracy, three, started the machinery that put the mill back in operation.

Once the mill was running again, Winslow Williams turned his attention to construction of a mansion in Yantic. The house, called Rockclyffe, sat on the top of what is now called Mansion Hill. By 1870, E. Winslow Williams

Woolen manufacturer E. Winslow Williams lived on Broadway before moving his family to this house, which he named Rockclyffe. *Courtesy of Yantic Fire Engine Company No. 1.*

was living in Yantic with assets totaling $125,000 real estate, more than $32 million today.

Although he had moved his family four or five miles from the center of the city, Winslow Williams remained active in city affairs. Both Winslow and his father were directors of the Farmers' and Mechanics' Savings Bank. Also like his father, Winslow served as a trustee and incorporator of Norwich Free Academy. He also was president of the Norwich Foot Ball Club, organized in 1881 for competition with teams in other communities.

About 1877, the mill was incorporated as the Yantic Woolen Company, a stock corporation, with Winslow Williams serving as its first president for the eleven years until his death.

WINSLOW TRACY (W.T.) WILLIAMS (1863–1930)

As the eldest son, Lewis B. Williams was the heir apparent to succeed his father at the mill and, at twenty-four, had already become superintendent. His death in 1884 shifted the mantle to his brother's shoulders, and when their father died in 1888, Winslow Tracy Williams withdrew from Yale without returning for senior year and became the third generation of his family to run the Yantic Woolen Mill.

W.T. Williams was born in Norwich but spent most of his life in Yantic; the family moved to Rockclyffe when he was five. W.T. Williams not only continued his father's tradition of looking after and financially supporting the Yantic Fire Company but also was actively involved, serving as foreman and also as engineer.

In 1889, W.T. Williams went to New York to marry Florence Prentice, daughter of William Packer and Florence (Kelly) Prentice. Their two children were born in Norwich.

In addition to running the mill, W.T. Williams was an active presence in Norwich city and town affairs. He was president of the W.W. Backus Hospital and a director of the Chelsea Savings Bank. When it was time for the city's 250th-birthday celebration, he was not only a member of the planning committee but also chairman of the 250-member general committee that planned and executed the quarter-millennium celebration. He was also vice-chairman of the smaller executive committee.

Perhaps it was coincidence, but Williams might have been thinking ahead to the celebration as he built a stone bridge to replace the wooden structure

President William Howard Taft, *center*, was a guest of W.T. Williams, *right*, when he attended the city's 250th-anniversary celebration in 1909. *Courtesy of Yantic Fire Engine Company No. 1.*

that crossed the Yantic River to the residential area known as Sunnyside and Rockclyffe. A year later, President William Howard Taft would ride across that bridge in an open carriage to participate in the festivities for the 250th-anniversary celebration.

Although he had visited the city not long before, Taft was persuaded to visit Norwich by W.T. Williams, who went to the White House to call on his friend the president. The president would attend as long as the celebration date was changed to July to accommodate his schedule. The deal was sealed when Williams agreed the president would stay at Rockclyffe for the two days he would be in town. W.T. and Florence Williams hosted a breakfast for a large number of their friends and public officials to honor the president, who planted an oak tree—a "lineal descendant" of the storied Charter Oak—on the Rockclyffe grounds.

The Williams family maintained control of the mill until 1918, when they sold it to American Woolen Company. The mansion was part of the sale, so the Williams family moved to New York, where W.T. Williams died in 1930. American Woolen sold the mansion about ten years later, and it was razed.

W.T.'s son, Erastus, who also was on the fire department rolls, joined the army during the First World War. He was seriously wounded during the war and never returned to Yantic. Florence Prentice Williams was living with her unmarried daughter, Florence, in New York City until her death.

27

THE CARROLLS

From the time he was a young man, Lucius Carroll was a successful businessman. His broad range of business interests brought him a fortune but also benefitted the community.

LUCIUS W. CARROLL

69/257 Broadway

Lucius Carroll was a born merchant. At fifteen, he began working for Wiswall & Sanford in Webster, Massachusetts. Before he reached twenty-one, he owned a quarter share in the business and, on his own, was managing one of its stores. He went on to open his own store and made a fortune selling supplies to the many manufacturers of eastern Connecticut.

Lucius Wyman Carroll was born in Thompson, Connecticut, in 1815, the son of Wyman and Sarah (Crosby) Carroll. He began working for Wiswall & Sanford in Webster, Massachusetts, as an apprentice with a contract that stipulated he would be paid fifteen dollars if he stayed only one year, with an increase for additional years. Carroll stayed six years, and just before he turned twenty-one, he became a partner with one-quarter interest in the firm's three stores. The relationship continued until 1843, when Carroll left for Norwich to open a store selling manufacturers' supplies.

Manufacturers' supplier Lucius W. Carroll and his family lived at 257 Broadway until the 1980s. *Photo by the author.*

In 1843, Carroll married Charlotte Lathe Pope, the daughter of Charlotte (Lathe) and Jonathan Adams Pope, a wealthy Norwich manufacturer. The Carrolls were the parents of five children, two of whom died as children. A son was lost at sea as a young man.

L.W. Carroll & Co. was a commission merchant company that dealt in wool, cotton, manufacturers' supplies, dye stuffs, paint, oil and glass and was housed in one of the largest warehouses on Water Street in Norwich.

Carroll was also an original partner of the Occum Water Power Company and served as secretary and treasurer. He also owned a cotton mill in Griswold for about forty years. Carroll was also a director and vice-president of the Norwich Savings Society and president of the Quinebaug Bank and its successor, First National Bank. Additionally, Carroll was an original incorporator of Norwich Free Academy and a director of the Norwich Fire Insurance Company. He was an active member of Central Baptist Church.

Carroll was a Republican, but except for a term on the Norwich Board of Aldermen in 1859, he didn't seek political office. During the Civil War, by all accounts, Carroll was an active contributor to the cause.

In 1860, Carroll was well off, with combined assets totaled $27,000, but by 1870, the figure jumped to $150,000, making him an undeniably wealthy man.

Whether it was because they had more money or because an updating was needed, in 1871 Carroll decided to modernize the house by adding a French (mansard) roof, at an estimated cost of $2,500.

Carroll had taken partners in 1865, but by 1876, E.P. Jacobs had died and Captain Loren Gallup retired. Carroll's son Adams Pope Carroll joined the firm, prompting a name change to L.W. Carroll & Son.

In 1887, Carroll had a commercial building constructed at the intersection of Water and Main Streets as a real estate investment. Architect Stephen C. Earle had a challenge because the land drops off from Main to Water, but he designed a flatiron-shaped building with storefronts on two sides. The Carroll Building, as it came to be called, has been a landmark in downtown Norwich for many years.

When he died in 1900, Carroll was the oldest businessman on Water Street.

Adams Pope Carroll (1850–1935)

321 Broadway

Adams Pope Carroll was born in 1850 and educated at local schools and Norwich Free Academy, where he was valedictorian of the class of 1868. He graduated from Brown University and returned to Norwich to become a partner in his father's store.

He was a member of Central Baptist Church Board of Managers and a trustee of the Otis Library and also the Norwich Savings Society. He was a genealogist and researched the Carroll, Crosby, Pope and Adams families. At age sixty-five, he married the much younger Alice Miriam Fitz who had been a dietician at William W. Backus Hospital and instructor in household economy at Bates College.

They lived about twenty years at 321 Broadway, the lovely brick house on the Corner of Carroll Avenue. Carroll died in 1935 while at their home in Crescent Beach, Niantic. Alice apparently returned to Norwich and was residing in a Main Street apartment in 1940.

Adams Pope Carroll and his wife lived in this house at 321 Broadway, now the Levanto Alumni House on the Norwich Free Academy campus. *Courtesy of the author.*

GEORGE WYMAN CARROLL (1859–1936)

The youngest of the Carroll children, George Wyman, was born in 1859. He worked for the family firm but in 1902 entered the brokerage business. In 1884, he married Emma Frances Briggs, daughter of Lydia (Andrews) and the Honorable Ira Greene Briggs, a wealthy textile manufacturer in nearby Voluntown. Their son, George Wyman Jr. (1886), and his family continued to live at 257 Broadway until the 1980s.

28

ℐEREMIAH ℋALSEY

S tate representative Jeremiah Halsey was a key figure in construction of Connecticut's new state capitol, just as his grandfather had been seventy years before.

JEREMIAH HALSEY (1822–1892)

2/90 Broad Street

In 1871, the Connecticut General Assembly decided the state needed a new capitol building and named Jeremiah Halsey to the six-member commission to oversee construction of the new, gold-domed statehouse overlooking Bushnell Park in Hartford. Halsey was following in the footsteps of his grandfather, also named Jeremiah Halsey, who had built the old statehouse.

Halsey was born in 1822 in Preston, the son of Jeremiah Shipley and Sally (Brewster) Halsey. His father was a descendant of Thomas Halsey, founder of Southampton, New York; his mother was a descendant of William Brewster of the *Mayflower* settlers. His grandfather, a lawyer, was a Revolutionary War hero who fought with Ethan Allen at Fort Ticonderoga and was the first commissioned naval commander in the United States.

The elder Jeremiah and Andrew Ward of Guilford proposed to build the original statehouse, and as payment, they would receive proceeds

The Honorable Jeremiah Halsey, lawyer and legislator, lived at 90 Broad Street. *Photo by the author.*

from a lottery and the strip of land between Connecticut and New York known as the Connecticut Gore. The lottery was unsuccessful, and the title to the land proved imperfect. Instead of the wealth they apparently were hoping for, they ultimately accepted $20,000 against the $35,000 they spent on the construction.

The younger Jeremiah was a bit more fortunate in his statehouse construction experience. He might not have made any money, but he didn't lose any either, as he was also a member of the construction oversight commission for the new statehouse from 1873 to 1880.

Because he had a delicate constitution and impaired eyesight, young Jeremiah was educated at home and tried living in Georgia for the milder climate. He studied law and was admitted to the Georgia bar and then returned to Connecticut and was admitted to the bar in Windham County. About four years later, Halsey came to Norwich and went into partnership with Samuel C. Morgan. From 1863 to 1870, Halsey was admitted to the bar of the United States Circuit Court and the bar of the U.S. Supreme Court.

Although he was interested in public affairs, friends said he did not seek office—rather, the office sought him. Halsey was chosen to serve in the general assembly in 1852, 1853, 1859 and 1860. He was the Norwich City attorney from 1853 until he resigned in 1871 and also was corporation counsel from 1883 to 1888.

In 1854, Halsey married Elizabeth Fairchild, daughter of Andrew and Betsey Fairchild of Reading, Connecticut. They had no children.

Halsey was for many years a member of Christ Episcopal Church and served as vestryman and warden of the church. He also served on the board of trustees at Norwich Free Academy and was a director or adviser to all of the major educational and charitable institutions in the city.

In 1882, acknowledging his reputation and accomplishments as a lawyer, Trinity College conferred on him a doctor of law degree.

Jeremiah Halsey died at a Washington hotel on February 8, 1897—his seventy-fifth birthday—during the couple's annual winter visit to Washington, D.C.

29

CHRISTOPHER CRANDALL (C.C.) BRAND

H is name became his trademark, and his whale gun bomb lance made his name a household word among whale men around the globe.

CHRISTOPHER CRANDALL BRAND (1813–1875)

24/106 (East) Broad Street

In the days when buildings were lit with oil lamps, the name C.C. Brand was recognized the world over by seamen who hunted whales for their oil. Brand's factory on Franklin Street in Norwich produced guns that allowed sailors to fire their harpoons more safely and accurately.

C.C. Brand was born in 1813 in Rhode Island, the son of Captain Nathan and Eunice (Crandall) Brand. He married Temperance Allyn in 1835 in Groton.

His early training as a blacksmith provided the foundation for his later work. In 1852, C.C. Brand patented a whaling gun and bomb lance that was destined to take the "C.C. Brand" name around the world. Whalers found the new apparatus safer and more effective as they sought their quarry. The Brand whale gun replaced the uncertainty of thrusting a lance by allowing whalers to fire a rifle that would eject a lance and attached bomb from its barrel.

Above: Family members and servants turned out to greet Christopher C. Brand as he turned his carriage into his house at 106 Broad Street. *Courtesy of the Brand family.*

Right: Christopher C. Brand, namesake of the "C.C. Brand" trademark for whale guns. *Courtesy of the Brand family.*

Brand's factory opened on Franklin Street in 1860, and for the next twenty-seven years, the whale gun bomb lances would be taken around the world. They were said to be an especial favorite with the sailors of the Nantucket fleet. Brand's improved "whaling gun with bomb projectile" won an award at the American Centennial Exposition in 1876.

C.C. Brand was an original incorporator of Norwich Free Academy in 1853, but his name is notably absent from later listings of the town's eminent citizens. There is some family speculation that Brand was a proponent of states' rights during the Civil War, causing tension with the patriotic Unionist townspeople. This notion is perhaps reinforced by the appearance of Brand's name among the five citizens who sought a court injunction to keep the town from paying the cost of gunpowder used in the cannon salute to mark the Emancipation Proclamation that freed slaves in the Southern states on July 1, 1863.

Unlike many of the town's wealthy men, Brand was a Democrat and was active politically, both as a candidate for the common council and as a delegate to state conventions.

Brand was apparently interested in horticulture and was a vice-president of the New London County Horticultural Society. Several news articles throughout the 1860s tell of oversized fruit and vegetables he had grown, including strawberries measuring seven inches in diameter and a twelve-foot cornstalk that held at least eight ears of corn. He won notice for his grapes and vegetables in exhibitions and at the New London County Fair, where he also raced his horses.

He also apparently liked a good bet. In 1867, he bet $1,000 he could walk the thirteen miles from Norwich to New London. The 230-pound Brand walked eleven miles before he was overcome with dizziness and fell.

By 1860, the family lived at 26 East Broad Street. Ten years later, the family had expanded to include another generation. Son Junius; his wife, Minnie; and their ten-month-old daughter, Keokee, were enumerated with Brand, who was still a manufacturer. His eldest son, Christopher A. Brand, who was called "Kit," and his family lived next door for about ten years.

Daughter Josephine had married Henry A. Phelon, a naval officer and merchant, in 1865. After the war, Phelon returned to West Springfield, Massachusetts, where he was a merchant and postmaster. Later, he was appointed to a position in the Boston Customs House.

C.C. Brand died in 1875. After his death, the factory continued operation under his sons' management for another twelve years until the discovery of oil in the ground in Pennsylvania meant that whale oil was obsolete as a fuel for light. After Temperance Brand died in 1885, family members began to move. When the factory closed, Junius Brand became superintendent of the new Norwich Water Works. He moved to 167 Rockwell Street, where he lived with Minnie and four children. He died in 1927. Son Chauncey, who remained unmarried, was a machinist at the factory until at least 1887 and then moved to New London and worked at Fleischman's Yeast Co., returning in 1912 to Norwich just before he died.

Daughter Susan moved to West Springfield, Massachusetts, and was enumerated with her sister Josephine's family until she died in 1925. Kit Brand's widow and children also moved to West Springfield and lived next door. In 1880, Frederich, who was calling himself F. Ivanhoe Brand, was twenty-three and at home. He died, unmarried, six years later.

By 1894, the house on East Broad Street was owned by J.H. Woisard, proprietor of the National Bargain Store.

30

ꞪENRY ᗷILL

H is *History of the Bible* was a bestseller across the country, and at home, his Laurel Hill housing development brought rave reviews.

HENRY BILL (1824–1891)

74/270 Broadway

When Henry Bill bought his house on Broadway, it was the largest real estate transaction in the area in quite some time. For $25,000 cash, he bought the mansion and grounds, which were considered among the most elegant in the city. He was not only a book publisher but also a real estate investor and philanthropist.

Bill was born in northern Groton (now Ledyard) in 1824, the son of Gurdon and Lucy Bill. He attended Plainfield Academy and, following graduation, taught school in Plainfield and Groton. When he was twenty, his uncle James A. Bill, who lived in Lyme, Connecticut, offered Henry a job with his book publishing company in Philadelphia.

For three years, young Henry sold books door to door, the usual sales method of the time, and traveled throughout the West. In 1847, he returned to Connecticut and opened his own book publishing business in Norwich. Bill had the encouragement of the successful New York publishers, the

Henry Bill moved from Laurel Hill to this house at 270 Broadway. *Photo by the author.*

Harper brothers, who offered him an unlimited line of credit and remained his friends for the rest of their lives.

Books produced by Henry Bill Publishing were mainly about travel, religion or "scenes"—views of a particular locality. One of his bestsellers was *The History of the Bible*, edited by Reverend Alvan Bond, a well-known Norwich minister.

Henry Bill married Julia Octavia Chapman of Groton in 1847 and had seven children, four of whom died in childhood.

Like many others, Bill's fortune grew between 1850 and 1870, when the census showed assets totaling $200,000 ($52.8 million©). Bill's annual income in the mid-1860s had been $7,000, about $1.25 million©.

The family lived on Laurel Hill overlooking the Thames River, where Henry Bill and his partners had developed the area across the river from Norwich as a separate community with beautiful Victorian homes. Laurel Hill was eventually annexed to Norwich. The Bills' household included a housekeeper and a coachman.

Bill donated to the city a parcel of land now known as Laurel Hill Park. In his native Ledyard, he funded the library that bears his name and donated the Congregational parsonage.

By 1880, the family lived on Broadway in Norwich. When his health began to deteriorate, Bill reorganized the publishing firm as a joint-stock company, which continued its successful operation as Henry Bill Publishing Co., and he pursued other interests.

Bill was active in Norwich business and civic affairs. He was an initial incorporator of the Chelsea Savings Bank and its first vice-president, serving for more than twenty years. While not one of the original incorporators, Bill was an original donor to Norwich Free Academy. The Bills belonged to the Broadway Congregational Church.

Bill served a term in the state senate in 1853, and although he initially was a Democrat, he switched parties over the slavery issue and became an active Republican. He was a presidential elector in 1868.

During the Civil War, he put himself at the service of Governor Buckingham whenever called on. After the war, Bill was involved in the education of young African American men, one of whom became the editor of a newspaper in Georgia and another, a professor at Richmond University in Virginia.

In 1884, Florence Bill married Reverend Joseph Selden, son of Henry and Caroline Selden. The young Seldens had a son. In 1900, Jennie, who had become Jane, and her seventy-five-year-old mother were living at 270 Broadway with a staff that included a cook, a waitress, a servant and a trained nurse. Frederick Bill went into the paper manufacturing business and moved to Massachusetts, where he was a well-respected businessman and was known as a hunter and outdoorsman. He married Ella Sprague of Springfield in 1890.

31

EDWARD CHAPPELL

It should come as no surprise that Edward Chappell became a very wealthy man. He owned a lumber company at a time of huge growth in the city and sold coal to factories and railroads as they were growing as well.

EDWARD CHAPPELL (1815–1881)

75/161 Washington Street

Edward Chappell was born in 1815 in New London, the son of Ezra and Wealthy (Arnold) Chappell. He came to Norwich in 1837 and, three years later, opened the coal and lumber company, which grew until, at its peak, about forty men worked at its Central Wharf location. It was said it had 10 million feet of lumber and twenty thousand tons of coal in stock at any given time.

Chappell's wealth grew quickly, from $5,000 worth of property in 1850 to $75,000 in real estate and $275,000 personal estate in 1870—about $70.8 million[©] today.

In 1840, Edward Chappell married Mary H. Brewer of Norwich. Their daughter, Mary Brewer, was born on November 13, 1845, and her mother died two weeks later. Chappell married his sister-in-law Elizabeth Brewer in 1848.

When the census was taken in 1860, Chappell was living on lower Washington Street near his Brewer in-laws. He lived for a time on Fairmount Street on the west side of the Yantic River, but by 1872, he had moved to 75 (161) Washington Street, where he lived the rest of his life. The house is no longer standing.

Although perhaps not as active in the community as some of his peers, Chappell was a director of Second National Bank.

Mary Brewer Chappell married paper manufacturer Edwin Sanford Ely in 1872 and had four children. Julia Chappell, who never married, continued to live at 161 Washington Street until her death in 1899.

32

BELA LYON PRATT

One of the best-known sculptors of the early twentieth century spent his early years in Norwich, where he was fashioning tiny animals as a five-year-old. Bela Lyon Pratt was later hailed not only for his statues but also for the coins he designed for the U.S. Mint.

BELA LYON PRATT (1867–1917)

Rocklawn (Orchard and Beech Streets)

His mother said she couldn't keep beeswax (to strengthen thread) in her sewing basket because her son was using it for sculpture. As an adult, he became an accomplished sculptor whose work included statues and American coins.

Bela Lyon Pratt was born in 1867, one of the five children of George and Sarah (Whittlesey) Pratt. His father, a lawyer, came from South Weymouth, Massachusetts. His mother was born in Salem, Connecticut, where her father, Oramel Whittlesey, was the founder of the first music conservatory in the nation, the Music Vale Seminary.

In 1870, the family lived at Rocklawn, the estate on the hill above Broad Street, at the corner of Orchard and Beech Streets.

After George Pratt died in 1875, Sarah moved to Union Street, where she taught music. By 1900, she and daughter Gertrude had joined her son Oramel and his family in Kansas City.

Bela Pratt graduated from Yale and then studied at the Art Student League of New York (where he met Augustus Saint-Gaudens, the well-respected American sculptor, who became his mentor) and at École des Beaux-Arts in Paris.

When he returned to the United States, Pratt created sculptures at the World's Columbian Exposition in Chicago (1892) and the Pan-American Exposition in Buffalo, New York. (1906).

From 1893 to 1918, Pratt was head of the Sculpture Department at the School of the Museum of Fine Arts in Boston. While there, he modeled busts of Boston's intelligentsia, including Phillips Brooks of Trinity Church and Henry Lee Higginson, founder of the Boston Symphony Orchestra.

Pratt married Helen L. Pray of South Boston, Massachusetts, and they became the parents of four children.

Among Pratt's works are the representations of art and science at the entrance to the Boston Public Library and the statue of Nathan Hale in New London. Other works include the *Whaleman's Monument* in New Bedford, Massachusetts; *Edward Everett Hale* in the Boston Public Gardens; and *Andersonville Boy* on the grounds of the state capitol in Hartford. Pratt's work is part of the design of buildings such as the Library of Congress, Central Intelligence Agency and Department of Justice buildings in Washington, D.C. It is estimated that Pratt completed more than 180 works during a career that ended when he was forty-seven years old.

Pratt was the designer of the gold Indian Head half ($5.00) and quarter ($2.50) eagle coins, which are much coveted because they are the U.S. Mint's only coins with a recessed design.

33

PUBLIC BUILDINGS OF THE MILLIONAIRES' TRIANGLE

SLATER MEMORIAL MUSEUM (DEDICATED 1888)

108 Crescent Street

If the new Slater Memorial Museum had a slogan in 1886, it might have been "Beautiful art deserves a beautiful setting."

The museum was established as a memorial to John Fox Slater, donated by his son and successor, William A. Slater. As the owners of numerous textile mills with multiple other business interests, the Slaters were the wealthiest family in town.

William Slater had long been interested in art and had become a dedicated collector with a special interest in the Barbizon school of painting, purchased during the Slaters' trips to Paris and Biarritz.

Stephen C. Earle of Worcester, Massachusetts, was the architect commissioned to design the structure and oversee its construction. He used Monson granite from Massachusetts for the base, pressed brick for walls and brownstone terra cotta for trim. Everywhere in the building, there is something to be seen, whether carved animals at corners and in crevices, wooden flooring with alternating types of wood or carvings of terra cotta, brownstone or wood or mantles ornamented with carved dragons.

The Slater Museum is considered Earle's masterpiece work. Its Romanesque Revival design is in the style that has become known as

William A. Slater built the Slater Memorial Museum as a memorial to his father. *Courtesy of the author.*

Richardson Romanesque after Boston architect Henry Hobson Richardson, the nineteenth-century architect considered the best in America by his peers. The building was constructed at a cost of $150,000, (about $20.7 million©).

There is some suggestion that the building was originally to be an assembly hall and classroom building on the Norwich Free Academy campus, but the headmaster, Robert Porter Keep, persuaded Slater that an art museum would be valuable as a place where Norwich residents would be able to see works of art they might otherwise never view. Although that was a common approach among institutions in Europe, it was unheard of at a secondary school.

Slater was persuaded to provide an additional $80,000 for acquisition of more than two hundred plaster casts of Green and Roman classical statues.

The dedication ceremony in 1888 included an address by Norwich native Daniel Colt Gilman, president of Johns Hopkins University, who spoke on "Greek Art in a Manufacturing Town." Also on the platform was Reverend John P. Gulliver, a professor at Andover Theological Seminary, who organized the founding of NFA in 1853 while he was a minister in Norwich.

The Slater cast collection inspired other institutions to adopt the idea, and curator Henry Kent was called to consult in a half dozen cities. Even the august Metropolitan Museum of New York sent its committee on casts to Norwich. Slater sent a special railroad car to transport the group, which included renowned sculptor Augustus Saint-Gaudens and philanthropist Andrew Carnegie, and later entertained them at his home.

The first exhibition in the new museum was works from the Slaters' extensive collection and included works by Rembrandt, Millet and Rafaelli.

Over time, the museum's holdings grew to include what its promotional material describes as "a diverse array of fine and decorative art, historical artifacts and ethnographic material from five continents and 35 centuries."

Establishment of the Norwich Art School provided first-class instruction in the fine arts with the hope of training designed for local industries as well as artists. In 1906, a gift from manufacturer Charles A. Converse financed the addition of a gallery to show changing exhibits.

ST. PATRICK CATHEDRAL

213 Broadway

On Good Friday in 1871, a parade of 1,700 Irishmen with horse-drawn carts and wagons marched from the village of Greeneville to Broadway in Norwich. By Easter Sunday on April 9, they had dug the entire foundation of the new St. Patrick Church.

The beautiful Gothic church was designed by architect James Murphy of Providence, Rhode Island. For the last sixty years, it has been the cathedral church for the Roman Catholic Diocese

It took nearly eight years to build the magnificent church that is now St. Patrick Cathedral. *Courtesy of the author.*

of Norwich. In 2013, the church interior was restored and now resembles the edifice of the early years.

No Catholics lived in Norwich from its founding until 1831, but the next forty years brought a steady stream of immigrants seeking to escape harsh political conditions and the hunger of the potato famine in Ireland. The many factories in Greeneville provided opportunities for work, but by the mid-1860s, more than four thousand Catholics lived in the village, and its small Catholic church was seriously overcrowded. The solution was construction of a new church. Interestingly, the chosen site was adjacent to the homes of the wealthy mill owners who hired Irish servants. A short distance to the north, the Congregationalists were constructing a fashionable brownstone building to be called Park Congregational Church.

The cornerstone was laid on July 13, 1873, and it took another six years until the church opened. Meanwhile, parishioners were paying ten cents a week toward the costs of construction. The first Mass was said, using a temporary altar, on St. Patrick's Day in 1879. The formal dedication was on September 28, 1879. The adjacent school opened a short time later.

During the 1938 East Coast hurricane, damage at St. Patrick's included the namesake window, but the building was restored.

In 1952, St. Patrick's was consecrated as a cathedral for the newly formed Diocese of Norwich.

PARK CONGREGATIONAL CHURCH

283 Broadway

The third major nonresidential building of the Millionaires' Triangle is Park Congregational Church at the foot of Chelsea Parade, just across Crescent Street from Norwich Free Academy. When it opened in 1874, many of the town's influential citizens left Second Church and moved to the newly organized church, whose location was far more convenient to their homes.

Architect Stephen C. Earle designed a building that reflected its surroundings in its beauty and grace. The largest of the memorial windows were given by John F. Slater, Harriet Peck Williams and the family of David Smith.

Mrs. Williams presented the land for the church, which was across Broadway from her home and also gave the bell tower and clock, which

Park Congregational Church, organized in 1874, was designed by architect Stephen C. Earle. *Photo by the author.*

was installed not long before she died in 1880. At a church festival that year, friends told this riddle about the clock: "Why is it like its giver? Because it is full of good works." Mrs. Williams said a better answer would be, "Because it bears the marks of time on its face," said to be a typical display of her wit.

BIBLIOGRAPHY

Ballou, Adin, ed. *An Elaborate History and Genealogy of the Ballous in America.* Providence, RI: Press of E.L. Freeman & Son, 1888.

Beckford, William Hale. *The Leading Businessmen of Norwich and Vicinity, Embracing Greeneville and Preston.* Boston, MA: Mercantile Publishing Company, 1890.

Beers, J.H. & Co. *Commemorative Biographical Record of Tolland & Windham Counties.* Vol. 1. Chicago: J.H. Beers & Co., 1903.

Buckingham, Samuel Giles. *The Life of William A. Buckingham: The War Governor of Connecticut.* Springfield, MA: W.F. Adams, 1894.

Campbell, W.H.W. *Memorial Sketch of Lafayette S. Foster: United States Senator from Connecticut, and Acting Vice-President of the United States.* Boston, MA: Franklin Press; Rand, Avery, & Co., 1881.

Caulkins, Frances Manwaring. *History of Norwich, Connecticut: From Its Possession by the Indians to the Year 1866.* Chester, CT: Pequot Press, 1976.

Children of William Parkinson and Augusta E. Greene. *The Greene Family in England and America: With Pedigrees.* Boston, MA: privately printed (T.R. Marvin & Son, Printers), 1901.

Connecticut Historical Commission. "Historical and Architectural Survey of Downtown Norwich." Hartford, CT, 1981. http://www.askncdc.com/planning/documents/HistoricResourcesInventory.pdf.

Dana, Malcolm McGregor. *The Norwich Memorial: The Annals of Norwich, New London County, Connecticut in the Great Rebellion of 1861–65.* Norwich, CT: J.H. Jewett and Company, 1873.

Huntington, Samuel, and Richard Thomas Huntington. *The Huntington Family in America: A Genealogical Memoir of the Known Descendants of Simon Huntington from 1633–1915*. Hartford, CT: Hartford Printing Company, 1915.

Hurd, D. Hamilton. *History of New London County, with Biographical Sketches of Many of Its Pioneers and Prominent Men*. Philadelphia, PA: J.W. Lewis & Co., 1882.

Marshall, Benjamin Tinkham. *A Modern History of New London County*. Vols. 1–3. New York: Lewis Historical Company, 1922.

National Park Service Eastern Office, Division of Design and Construction. Historic American Buildings Survey HABS No. CONN-251. Philadelphia, PA, 1960.

Officer, Lawrence H., and Samuel H Williamson. "Measures of Worth," Measuring Worth 2012. www.measuringworth.com/worthmeasures.php.

Perkins, Mary Elizabeth. *Old Houses of the Antient Town of Norwich 1660–1800*. Norwich, CT: Bulletin Company, 1895.

Roosevelt, Edith Kermit Carow. *American Backlogs: The Story of Gertrude Tyler and Her Family, 1660–1860*. New York: C. Scribner's Sons, 1928.

Salzer, Dick. "The Norwich Gun Industry." Norwich Historical Society. http://norwichhistoricalsociety.org/resources/pdfs/90_saltzer_norwich.pdf.

AVAILABLE AT OTIS LIBRARY REFERENCE DEPARTMENT

Norwich Newspapers, including the *Bulletin*, *Aurora* and *Courier*. Various dates throughout the 1800s and early 1900s.

Steadman's Norwich Directory. Various years, 1861–1900s.

ꟾNDEX

About the Author

Tricia Staley is a retired high school administrator and history teacher. Before teaching, she was a newspaper reporter and editor in Massachusetts and Connecticut for fifteen years.

Tricia has a BA in history from the University of Massachusetts–Amherst and holds advanced degrees from Sacred Heart University in Fairfield, Connecticut. In addition, she holds certificates in genealogical studies and American maritime history.

She is a member of the board of directors of the Friends of Slater Memorial Museum in Norwich, Connecticut, and belongs to the Norwich Historical Society, the Connecticut Society of Genealogists and Mystic Seaport Museum, where she also volunteers.

Tricia has presented Millionaires' Triangle Walking Tours, featuring many of the subjects covered in this book, for the Slater Museum's docent training and the Last Green Valley's Walktober event.